LOTTERY WINNERS

LOTTERY WINNERS

How They Won and How Winning
Changed Their Lives

H. ROY KAPLAN

HARPER & ROW, PUBLISHERS
NEW YORK, HAGERSTOWN
SAN FRANCISCO
LONDON

FIRST EDITION

DESIGNED BY SIDNEY FEINBERG

Library of Congress Cataloging in Publication Data

Kaplan, H. Roy.
    Lottery winners.
    1. Lottery winners—United States. I. Title.
HG6126.K36   920'.073   78-2143
ISBN 0-06-012257-9

---

78 79 80 81 82 10 9 8 7 6 5 4 3 2 1

To my parents and Mary, Eric, and Ian

Contents

Acknowledgments

Seven years ago Dr. Carlos Kruytbosch of the National Science Foundation and I conceived a study to ascertain the strength of the commitment to work in the United States. Big lottery winners were focused on, since for them the economic incentive for working was removed. Little did I realize then that this project would occupy so much of my time, be fraught with so many frustrations, and develop into this volume. I am grateful to Dr. Kruytbosch for his assistance in the formative stages of this project and for his encouragement and support. I would also like to express my appreciation to Dr. Elliot Liebow of the National Institute of Mental Health for his encouragement to continue when I was about to quit. Thanks are also extended to the many lottery officials around the country who assisted me in collecting information. I owe a special debt of gratitude to Ms. Jo Tursi and Jack Taylor, affiliated with the New Jersey State Lottery.

Preliminary work on the study was assisted by a grant from the Research Foundation of the State University of New York, and the preparation of the manuscript was supported by a grant from the Research and Development Committee of Pitzer College. I appreciate the encouragement, tolerance, and understanding of my eccentric behavior from my colleagues in the Department of Sociology at the State University of New York at Buffalo. I also wish to thank Professor Kenneth Joyce of the Law School at that university for his assistance in clarifying aspects of inheritance-tax law.

Patricia Kimball and Nancy Cone gave me valuable editorial suggestions. To Cy Chermak go my thanks for giving the project a boost when it counted, and to the scores of winners who allowed me to speak with them go my heartfelt thanks.

My parents and mother-in-law helped make the field work more bearable and I am grateful for their warm meals and shelter. The weeks away from my wife and children during the years of field work can never be regained, but their support, understanding, and encouragement gave me the impetus to complete this work.

"A lifetime of happiness! No man alive could bear it: it would be hell on earth."

—GEORGE BERNARD SHAW,
Man and Superman

LOTTERY WINNERS

Introduction

THE PLACE: The Garden State Arts Center in Holmdel, New Jersey.
THE TIME: Fall 1972.

Three thousand people are in the audience and more are arriving for the concert scheduled to begin at 8:30. But the focus of the crowd's attention is already on the stage, where several people are hovering around a spinning drum containing little red balls with names inside them. Everyone is waiting anxiously, eagerly anticipating the final drawing which will reveal the newest instant millionaire in the New Jersey State Lottery. In the crowd are seventy-five finalists who have come from as far away as Los Angeles in search of fame and fortune. The smaller prizes of $10,000, $100,000, and $200,000 have already been won. Their hopes rest on winning the final prize, the big one. It is a long shot—twenty million to one—and, yet, they have already defied the laws of probability by making it this far. Why not all the way? Why not steal the whole show?

Liberace, the guest celebrity, reaches into the drum, pulls out a ball, and hands it to the Master of Ceremonies. Inside is the name that everyone is waiting to hear. Who will it be?

"The newest member of the New Jersey millionaire club is . . . Salvatore Lenochi."

"I couldn't believe my ears. I thought I was hearing things. I got so excited when I heard my first name that I shouted and wasn't sure what the last name was. The next thing I knew, I was up on the stage in front of all those people and Liberace was shaking my hand and wishing me good luck. I don't even remember driving home. I lived sixty miles away and I must have been doing a hundred all the way."

It is three years later. The applause has faded, Sal is now thirty-eight, and his wife is expecting their fourth child. They live in a new $100,000 nine-room, two-story home on four acres in a farming area in central New Jersey. There is a $4,000 pool in the backyard alongside a kennel and a small barn. A Continental Mark IV is parked in the driveway. As we spoke, Sal munched on some pig's knuckles at the kitchen table. His wife, Jan, stayed out of sight in the den.

"I remember how it was then. I didn't even have a good suit to wear to the drawing. I used safety pins to hold my pants up. They were attached to my shirt. When I won, I put my arms around my wife to kiss her, and the pins ripped right through the shirt. Now I have the money and I'm not sure if I wasn't better off before.

"Jan won't talk to anyone about it and she doesn't want me to discuss it. She's still upset. It was terrible. Reporters hounded us. They were even inside our kids' school looking for them. The kids were the ones who really suffered. They had their pockets turned inside out and knives pulled on them. I was afraid somebody would try and kidnap them, and I'm still scared about it. We don't have the money for a ransom. People are being driven to do funny things these days.

"Ever since the day we won, it's brought problems. Our phone rang for forty-eight straight hours. It started at six in the morning. There were well-wishers, crank calls, and all sorts of nuts. One guy called from Jersey City. He said his wife had no legs and was in bed. He wanted money for artificial limbs for her and a little money for himself to live on. He said we should send it in the mail. A few days later, he called and said the money hadn't come. 'It wasn't in the mail. Where is it?' After that he would call every day.

"Things got rough at my grocery store, too. People were coming in to see me and touch me, to shake my hand, rub me for luck. Some actually claw you. People used to see me and shout it out, 'Here comes the millionaire!' It got so bad, I used to dress up like a bum to avoid being spotted and get some peace. I didn't shave or nothing. It's really unfair. My nextdoor neighbor was a businessman and he makes more than $50,000 a year and no one bothers him. They used to drive by and stop in front of our house. Even today, if I go to my sister's house and a friend comes in, right away they want to see the 'millionaire.' They even bothered my brother. He went on a trip to California and airport personnel stopped him when he got off the plane. They thought he was me. Anyone that finally finds out, you get a different treatment.

"People's attitudes about you change, too. People come in different grades. First there were the well-wishers. Then came the hand-shakers trying to rub off luck. Then there were those who were resentful and envied you. And then there were those who began fabricating stories about you. Some began saying I won twice, and there was a story going around that I had a yacht. Finally, there were the people who would walk away from you. They feel they can't compete with you. One woman drove more than half an hour to get to my home to personally insult me. She said I was part of the machine. That my name was selected beforehand. She said she had been buying tickets for years and never won and that's how she knew it was fixed.

"The money even created tensions in my family. It's a quiet tension—an undercurrent. You know it's there and you just accept it. For example, I was at my sister's house and her faucet was dripping. I said, 'Your faucet is leaking. You ought to have it fixed.' She said, 'Well, if I had your money, I'd fix it.'

"It does affect your life, there's no doubt about that. Socially and in every other way. Before I won, I used to blow up at people if they deserved it. Now I don't. If I did, people would say I act like that because I have the money. You have to take a lot of guff. It puts you in a shell. We haven't even had a vacation. Last summer I won $25 in the lottery and I waited for four months before I got up the nerve to go cash it in. There was no place I could go in the city where I could blend in.

"Finally, I threw in the towel and sold my grocery store. It wasn't doing well. My brothers and I shared in the profits and I was only making about $9,000 a year and working seventy hours a week. Moving didn't bother the kids. They wanted us to move. They even lie for us. They've been through hell and they don't want anybody to know. Out here nobody knows, and that's the way I want to keep it. We've got good neighbors here. I don't want anything to hinder these relationships. Sure, some of them are suspicious. They ask me why I'm home so much and what type of work I do. I guess they wonder how I am able to own such a nice house without working. We have to justify everything we do. We'd like to go on a trip to California, but if we go, I'd have to explain it.

"I'm going to college now, studying to become an accountant, but it's not easy. I studied twelve to fourteen hours a day in the beginning of the semester before I got used to the new routine. But I would go out of my mind if I didn't go to school. I like to work, the challenge of it. In a way, I miss working, but I'm not going back to what I did before, and right now I'm not taking chances on anyone recognizing me and asking questions. I'm looking forward to the day when I'll be an accountant. Even though they're going to take most of it in taxes, I still want to work. If the government's going to take fifty percent from my job, I want something I can enjoy. In a way, I guess you can say that winning the money has been an advantage. I can take an interesting job with growth potential and it doesn't have to pay well, but I wouldn't want to win again. That would be a nightmare!"

For many people like Sal Lenochi, winning a fortune in the lottery is the one dream that has a possibility, however remote, of coming true. Whether the prize be $25,000 or a million dollars, they are convinced that winning would relieve them of financial worries forever and magically propel them into the glamorous lives of the beautiful people they have read about in magazines or seen in the movies and on TV. For the man struggling to make his mortgage payments and keep his car from the finance company, or the widow eking out an existence on inadequate Social Security payments, the lottery is the grist of which fantasies are made.

This book is about people who won, what happened to them and their families, how they used the money, how their lives have changed, and how other people have changed toward them. The material was derived from interviews with more than 100 big-money winners in New York, Pennsylvania, Illinois, Maryland, and New Jersey. Unlike journalistic reports which are based on brief conversations with a few outgoing winners, it grew out of a conscientious effort to contact all million-dollar winners in New Jersey, the first state to have a regular million-dollar lottery. In all, one third of the million-dollar winners in the United States were interviewed. The work was arduous, taking four years and 15,000 miles of driving and complicated by winners' reluctance to be interviewed. I began by speaking with forty-five of the fifty $50,000 and $100,000 winners in western New York, and then turned to the $250,000 and million-dollar winners in New Jersey. Ultimately, thirty-three of the thirty-seven New Jersey millionaires were contacted, many for the first time. Since nearly the entire population of winners was studied, we can assume that the experiences they had would, in all probability, be like ours if we won.

The study, as originally conceived by Dr. Carlos Kruytbosch of the National Science Foundation and myself, sought to discover whether or not people continue working after the economic incentive for doing so is removed. The interviews averaged three hours, and many ran more than four. As they progressed, the winners shared a great deal of information. Once convinced of my sincerity, they poured out their pent-up emotions and discussed previously undisclosed problems, fears, and experiences. Some accounts were so fascinating and extraordinary that I decided to bring them together into this volume. Although the stories may seem bizarre, they were experiences of typical lottery-ticket buyers, and studies indicate that buyers do not differ from the general public except they are slightly older, and as many as eighty percent of the adult population in lottery states buys tickets.*

Since many people feared and shunned public exposure, pseudonyms are used to protect their identities. Their reluctance stemmed from the traumatic experiences they had had or anticipated, experiences which often created barriers between them and their families, friends, and society. One of the first shocks resulted from being thrust into the limelight, scrutinized by the mass media, and eyed by con men and shysters around the world. Many winners were bombarded with mail. There were good wishes, bad wishes, thinly veiled sexual propositions, marriage proposals (one elderly widow had received twenty-five at last count), solicitations for loans, investment schemes, and outright requests for money by churches, clubs, charities, destitute individuals—even two drum-and-bugle corps. Some communications bordered on the absurd, but others were ominous. Threats and the fear of extortion attempts forced many winners, especially those with young children, to isolate themselves. Thirty millionaires moved in order to maintain privacy and insulate themselves from a potentially hostile world.

*Only two winners were nonwhites. There were no black million-dollar winners in New Jersey until recently. Blacks are not frequent patrons of the lottery, preferring instead to play the numbers—a game which has become institutionalized in their subculture from tradition, its accessibility, and its nontaxable nature.

Friends' motives often became suspect and their behavior was said to change, but winners less often recognized the subtle changes in their own behavior. When they moved, they usually did not tell their new neighbors about their good fortune. If the subject was raised, they would deny it, even fabricating intricate stories to allay suspicion.

Relationships within winners' families were often strained, too. Children frequently expected more than they received, and long-lost relatives suddenly appeared anticipating a share. There were even cases of marital discord which, though probably nascent before the win, were exacerbated by it.

Most winners might be described as working-class, having a wide variety of jobs but, with few exceptions, low earnings. It was ironical that, now that they were financially secure, many were constrained in their spending. Their self-imposed isolation prevented them from enjoying the spoils of their victory over poverty. Loneliness was something many millionaires had to contend with, especially those who bought homes in remote places or tried to keep their secret. A continuation of normal routine meant girding for the inevitable onslaught of calls and interviews by reporters, friends, neighbors, and solicitors. The pressure was so intense that some people had to leave their jobs because of actual or anticipated harassment from supervisors, co-workers, and customers.

One of the more interesting aspects of winners' behavior was their anticipatory anxiety and fear. Even when they had not been harassed, they knew of someone like Sal who had, so many withdrew to live in a climate of fear and mistrust. In addition to the loss of belonging to their community, there was a concomitant feeling of estrangement from and hostility toward the government because their winnings were heavily taxed. They often received less than half the amount advertised (this is true even of millionaires who receive twenty annual installments of $50,000), and many people felt harassed by the Internal Revenue Service.

Although most people expect Uncle Sam to take a sizable chunk, there are those, like Loren Porter, who are devastated by it. Loren was a short-haul truckdriver when he won $100,000 in the New York State Lottery in 1968. He quit his job and invested in a construction company that he and an acquaintance founded. The business soured and his partner skipped town, leaving him with little capital and a lot of bills. The *coup de grace* arrived in the form of a reminder from the IRS that he had not yet paid the government its share of the winnings—$61,000. This tax left him penniless, unemployed, and in debt. "I was so run-down from grief I just wanted to kick the bucket. I didn't know whether I was coming or going. I was in a fog for at least a year."

To satisfy creditors, Loren sold most of his worldly possessions, including the Cadillac he had bought, and moved into a decaying house trailer on a hillside in the woods. A series of articles in a local newspaper stirred public indignation and gained a promise of an IRS review to see that "every nickel of tax savings that he might be entitled to is found." This exhaustive audit netted a refund of $300. Currently, he is doing the thing he knows best: driving a truck. "It's a good thing I went back to work or I wouldn't have been able to take it. It gave my mind a place to go." Today he stridently avoids discussing his win: "It bothers me whenever I think about it. All I want to do is forget."

Several winners found themselves assessed hundreds of additional dollars after speaking about their finances to the mass media, a result which solidified a later resolve to remain uncommunicative. Despite their attempts to maintain privacy, winners were invariably found out, and some moved several times in a desperate drive to achieve anonymity. With the moves came other kinds of threats and challenges. Living in posh suburbs, they wondered if they would be accepted, how they would explain their affluence, and always there was the gnawing fear of being recognized.

Since most millionaires quit their jobs, they were often home. How could they explain their source of income without revealing their secret? More important, what would they do with their newly won freedom? These questions persisted through days and months, even years after winning. As they grappled with their new economic status, they realized that their lives would never be the same; that their old jobs were gone, along with their former routines. They contemplated alternative life-styles, but were ill-equipped to handle their new circumstances. Today some wander aimlessly through life, squandering their annual installments.

To cope with the quirk of fate which wrested them from a marginal existence, or perhaps to lend some purpose to the madness of the events that transformed their lives, winners frequently attributed their good luck to divine intervention. Many people prayed to God for small amounts and reported winning shortly thereafter. In a similar intriguing vein were the large number of people who reported having psychic experiences. Dreams, premonitions—even voices—were channels commonly believed to have alerted them to or influenced their wins.

There is a natural curiosity about how many tickets winners buy and where they purchase them. The answers to these questions are here, as are revelations about what they do with their time and money. We learn that, once free of the economic necessity of working, at first they revel in their security, but years afterward they are looking for something to occupy their time. Few have embarked on new careers, developed other interests, or tried to realize fantasies harbored before winning. Their lives are often filled with nostalgia for the "good old days" that were free of high mortgage payments, tax problems, and fear. Come share their experiences, the good and the bad, which provide a glimpse of what it is like to get your hands into the pot of gold at the end of the rainbow.

CHAPTER 2

The Winners and How They Did It: Gambling, Luck, and Psychic and Religious Experiences

"If you want to know what God thinks of money,
look at the people he gives it to."
—*Old New England Saying*

It is late afternoon on a Thursday in October. The place is a rustic New York tavern in a valley not far from the Pennsylvania border. Inside, half a dozen construction workers huddle around one end of the bar quaffing beer. The door opens and a lean, disheveled man carrying a small paper bag enters, saunters up to the group, and withdraws a long strand of Pennsylvania State Lottery tickets. The men eagerly dig into their pockets for dollar bills. Within a few minutes, fifty tickets are snapped up and the stranger leaves. The conversation turns to the New York lottery as they begin buying sheets of tickets from the bartender, who is a franchised agent. Above the cash register hangs an incentive booster—a sign proclaiming that a $500 winning ticket was sold there last week.

This scene is repeated daily in thousands of places around the country. Fourteen states (New Hampshire, New York, New Jersey, Pennsylvania, Connecticut, Maryland, Rhode

Island, Massachusetts, Delaware, Maine, Ohio, Illinois, Vermont and Michigan) hold lotteries. In department stores, supermarkets, restaurants, gas stations, banks, and myriad other locations, tickets are hawked and the public is lured with the offer of instant wealth. The odds against winning big money are astronomical—the buyer generally has a better chance of being struck by lightening or bitten by a shark while swimming in the Hudson River. Nevertheless, ticket sales are brisk among would-be millionaires.

And there are winners, thousands of them around the country. They have won everything from 100 feet of hot dogs to a year's supply of groceries; from motorcycles to Cadillacs; from trailers to luxury homes; from trips to Disneyland to around-the-world cruises; and from $5 to several million dollars. How do they do it? What is their secret? These questions cross the minds of millions of losers each week when the pictures of jubilant new millionaires are plastered across the front pages of newspapers. There are even slick publications that hold out tantalizing plans on how to play the lottery game, as if there were some secret technique that might reduce the enormous odds. Many people think buying a lot of tickets increases their chances of winning. A few years ago *The New York Times* carried the story of a college finance officer who "invested" several hundred dollars in tickets in the hope of relieving the financial pressure on the college. Needless to say, he didn't win. The odds are so stacked against winning that buying extra tickets cannot appreciably tip them in your favor. But you cannot persuade inveterate lottery patrons that it is fruitless to hedge their bet.

Martin Weil of the *Washington Post** reported one of the largest amounts ever wagered in a lottery. The bet was placed by seventy-two-year-old Henry Foffman in the Maryland daily lottery, a legalized numbers game which allows bettors to pick their own number. Foffman had won between $50,000 and $60,000 on Fridays whose dates included the

*February 4, 1978.

number 3, and on February 3, 1978, following a "lucky" hunch, he placed $10,000 on number 311, paying for the wager in $10,000 worth of his uncashed winning tickets. The 500-to-1 odds would have yielded five million dollars. When word of the huge wager spread, an additional $2,000 was placed on the number. The lottery commission halted betting on it when the possible winnings equaled the lottery's six-million-dollar reserve fund. Foffman, who had hedged his bet by placing $1,000 on like numbers, remained at the Baltimore shoe store where he purchased the tickets to watch his dream of instant riches vanish before him on the televised drawing.

The most concerted, calculated, and expensive effort to beat a lottery was made in 1977 by Mr. and Mrs. Tom Drake, a couple in their twenties who live in Pennsylvania. Over a period of four months they spent $14,100 on tickets. This netted them a $10,000 prize, two $1,000 prizes, and lesser amounts of $100, $25, and $5. Their total winnings amounted to $15,000, and their 16,000 chances gave them 1,203 qualifiers for the semifinal drawings from which 100 people are selected as finalists for the million-dollar grand prize. The Drakes researched the mechanics of the Pennsylvania lottery, learning that one finalist ticket is drawn for every 40,-000 qualifiers. They saved their qualifiers for the last drawing and dramatically decreased the odds, but, alas, lost. And although it appeared they had broken even, their lost wages amounted to more than $6,000. Nevertheless, they viewed the experience as rewarding. It allowed them to leave onerous jobs and rejuvenated their marriage. They have embarked on new careers and have signed contracts with various media, receiving several thousand dollars from *Good Housekeeping* for the story of their brush with Lady Luck.

The practice of multiple ticket purchasing was encouraged in New York when tickets were sold in a series of five and players were informed that one letter of the series would be selected as the first entry on the winning ticket. What was not emphasized was the fact that the six numbers also had to match. It later turned out that the odds against winning were nearly doubled, since the state was including unsold tickets in the drawing and nearly half the jackpots were never awarded because they went to ownerless tickets. When this fact was publicly revealed, the lottery was halted and the entire staff of over 300 replaced in a reorganization.

Ticket-buying habits of winners vary widely. Some purchase a set number religiously each week, while others buy tickets infrequently. In fact, I spoke with three million-dollar winners who had bought only one or two tickets in their lives. One New Jersey millionaire proudly proclaimed, "I just bought two a week for six months before I won. It cost me only $24." Such cases are, however, the exception. Nearly all the winners I interviewed bought tickets regularly before they won, averaging four a week. The most any one spent was $15 a week.

Winners come from a variety of locations ranging from rural to urban areas, from small towns to big cities. There have been periods when a particular geographic area yielded an inordinate number of winners, as in western New York several years ago with $50,000 winners. "This confirms," said a middle-aged winner, "what I and my friends have known for a long time: Buffalo is going to become the psychic capital of the world."

Since we are dealing with probabilities, things have a way of evening out, and high-win areas eventually have a dry spell. But there have been some extraordinary coincidences, such as the case of Betty Rawlins and her friend Elenore Ratkowski. They live in a sparsely populated region of western New York referred to as the Southern Tier. One day, five years ago, they met unexpectedly at a local supermarket. As Mrs. Ratkowski describes it:

"We were shopping together, and, knowing that Betty wasn't feeling well, I let her ahead of me at the checkout counter. She bought a lottery ticket and won $100,000 with it. That would have been my ticket if I hadn't let her in ahead of me. But I had no ill feelings. I only wished her well."

Later, almost five years to the day, Elenore Ratkowski won $114,000 from a ticket purchased at the same store. A similar situation occurred in Buffalo when next-door neighbors won $50,000 six months apart.

Just as the locales of winners vary, so do the places where winning tickets are purchased. There are literally thousands of agents throughout the fourteen states that hold lotteries, and big winners have bought tickets at such diverse places as bars, restaurants, banks, and gas stations. Many winners purchased tickets from associates at work, and this often created problems for them. A number of them gave the sellers a cash bonus ranging from $100 to $2,000.

Licensed ticket agents get a commission equivalent to one percent of the winning tickets they sell. But for two vendors there was an added bonus: they sold winning tickets to themselves. Jan Story had thirty tickets left over from his allotment and purchased them because he "felt lucky." This was a good hunch because one of them netted him $50,000. Diana and Jim Farley hit an even bigger bonanza—a million dollars with a ticket they purchased in their own grocery store in central New Jersey. An elderly couple with meager income, they wasted little time in retiring and moving to Florida, their future considerably more secure.

It is true that some agents have had more than their share of winners, but this is undoubtedly because they sell a large volume of tickets. One large supermarket in northern New Jersey has sold two million-dollar tickets and, unknown to many patrons of the store, both winners were employees.

Scientifically, all that can be said about these events is that they are coincidences. Yet, the public revels in such mysteries and seeks out lucky people and the places they frequent in the hope that some of the luck will rub off on them. This practice has impelled winners to quit their jobs and even move in an attempt to maintain their privacy. The superstitious beliefs of the public can be carried to extremes. Big winners received numerous requests to purchase tickets for strangers, including letters containing money. Many winners were asked to touch or handle tickets so their luck might rub off. One custom, the "rubbing ritual," was particularly offensive. Winners were often mobbed, rubbed, and touched for luck so much so that some were bruised, mauled, and clawed. A seventeen-year-old high-school girl was subjected to this after she won a million dollars:

"The day after I won, I went to school and there were reporters all over. People were crowding around me, pushing me, trying to touch me. When I got in the building, I was red all over."

Few winners were habitual gamblers before they won; aside from bingo and an occasional card game, most rarely wagered. Several people journeyed to Las Vegas to see if their luck would continue, but in most cases it did not.

One notable exception was a million-dollar winner who hit a $650 jackpot in a slot machine. "I wasn't dressed very well and the noise attracted a crowd. A woman near me turned to a friend and said, 'He's not even excited.' Another looked at me and said, 'I'm sure glad that poor man won.' As we left, I turned to my wife and said, laughing, 'If they only knew!' "

Success has not dampened the winners' enthusiasm for the lottery; most buy more tickets now than before. Many have extended their purchases into other states, because "it's something to do" or "the money is for education." One man said half-seriously, "I'm giving it back to them, slowly."

To many winners, buying tickets is a challenge—to defy the odds by repeating. But the probability of this happening is infinitesimal. Yet, some people win often. In upstate New York I interviewed a $50,000 winner who regularly collects. "I've won money and free tickets in the lottery many times. Twice I've hit for $50 and once for $100 and $1,000. When I went down to the redemption center, I said, 'It's me again.' "

Lottery officials in New Jersey related the story of a man who has been in the finals for a million dollars four times, but unfortunately has never won big. Another man from New Jersey won a $10,000 consolation prize in the finals. Six months later he won $200,000 and another $10,000 *on the same day.* At one of the drawings I attended, a woman was a finalist for $250,000. Two years before, she had had a winning $50,000 ticket which was stolen. She approached this drawing believing she was being given another chance and took away $10,000.

At times it seems that fate is indeed fickle. As poverty and misery seem to plague some families, so, too, luck seems to run in others. Six millionaires reported missing the finals for a second million-dollar drawing by one number, and many others won smaller amounts on many occasions. Two of them had uncles who won $50,000 within a year after their own scores.

Some people claim to be very lucky—for example, Sandy Lyons, a foundry worker in Buffalo. Four years ago Sandy won $50,000, and he has won lesser amounts on several other occasions.

"I'm blessed, I guess. I've always been lucky. Once in a while I get a premonition or have a dream and I follow it and it comes out right. I've been playing the lottery since it started and I told my wife I'd win. I'm still buying tickets and I know I'm going to hit it again."

Laymen call it luck; scientists refer to it in terms of probabilities. Depending upon your preference, there can be no doubt that some people have had phenomenal success in lotteries, defying the law of probability. One of the most unusual cases involved Marty Timmons. Two years ago he qualified twice in the finals of the New Jersey lottery with the same ticket and won two large prizes: first, $10,000 and then, an hour later, a million. It is not unusual for someone to qualify for two prizes with one ticket, but this was the first time anybody hit the jackpot as well as a consolation prize, and lottery officials were flabbergasted. Statisticians calculated the odds at *334 trillion to 1.*

"The first two and the last two numbers were identical, like 22 34 22. It gave me two chances. Still, I didn't think I would win. Boy, was I surprised! And, you know, it's funny how I came to buy that ticket.

"There's a guy I know from where I used to work. He buys tickets in New Jersey and sells them to the people at the plant. I buy two a week from him. Well, the week I bought the winning ticket, he had three left. Two of them he was saving for me. He just couldn't sell the last one. He went through the plant and tried to peddle it all day. There are over three hundred people that work there, and no one would buy it. My brother-in-law works there and told him, 'Take them up and see Marty, he'll buy them.' He did and I bought all three. That third one was the winner.

"You know, a funny thing happened to us before the drawing. A few days before, my wife was at a store and grabbed a handful of baseball bubblegum cards for my kids. The Sunday before the drawing, which was on a Wednesday, we were riding in the car and my kids [they have three] ate some of the gum. They left the cards and my wife stuffed them into her purse without looking. Monday night she opened her purse and found them there. One said, 'Something of great importance will happen to you the day after tomorrow,' and the other one said, 'You will soon inherit a vast fortune.' "

Marty and his wife looked upon this as a humorous coincidence, but many winners had similar experiences and took them seriously.

Betty Rawlins, the woman who purchased the ticket at the supermarket ahead of Elenore Ratkowski, did not buy it accidentally. She was persuaded by her granddaughter after an unusual experience.

"It happened when I was at my daughter's house. My granddaughter is very lucky, and she made me buy the ticket because she bought a horoscope and it said people born on my birthday should buy a lottery ticket. I never bought tickets before and I thought it was silly, but she insisted I do it. I still have the book."

She opened it to the page for her birthday, which revealed: "Money. Luck is with you. Take a chance; buy lottery tickets." It was the only citation in the book suggesting the purchase of lottery tickets.

Premonitions about winning were common and took many forms. Ed Powers, former director of the New Hampshire lottery, related the story of a finalist who lived in Los Angeles. "He called long distance before the drawing and said he wouldn't be able to come, but that we should mail him the $100,000. He didn't say it as a joke, he was positive that he'd win, and he did."

Sometimes people reported a physiological change which signaled success, as this million-dollar winner from New Jersey did. "I was sitting there beside my wife and I had a feeling that I was going to win. Just before they picked my name, my hands were funny. One was sweaty and red and the other was ice cold. I turned to my wife and said, 'We won.'"

One man had an inkling of his impending win, but ignored it. "I like to do a lot of hunting and fishing, and my friend and I were up in Canada ice-fishing. We were on the ice for forty-eight hours and didn't get a thing. Boy, was it cold! And all for nothing. As we packed up and started to leave, he said, 'We had such lousy luck, one of us is going to win the lottery.'

"I didn't think anything more about it. We drove home in a sleet storm, and after I got home my friend called up and said to check my tickets because one of us was the $50,000 winner. He knew because they published the number in the paper and we had a lot of tickets in sequence. My buddies and I would sit at the bar and throw in a dollar for tickets and flip for them. We'd buy a whole mess of them. I had twenty-two tickets that week.

"My wife said to check my tickets, but I was too tired. You know how you feel, that you're not going to win anyway. But she kept after me, so finally I checked and it was the first one I looked at. Right on top.

"Friends came over and we had a party. They all wanted to see the ticket, so I passed it around. I didn't even see it for over two hours, and then someone asked if I'd signed it and I realized I hadn't. You know, it was as though I passed out $50,000."

While most of this might be lumped under the heading of humorous anecdotes and coincidence, there were many incidents which were far more intriguing; events which could not be explained so easily. These are described in the remainder of this chapter in a context to provide a more detailed picture of individuals who had spiritual or psychic experiences.

Reports of an inner awareness or psychic communication which alerted them to their impending win were common. In several instances this experience was believed to be the result of extrasensory perception (ESP) which directed people like William Lawrence to locations where they felt compelled to purchase tickets.

Bill lives with his wife, Pauline, in a small modern apartment in the business section of a Buffalo suburb. He is sixty years old and has worked as a metallurgist in a local factory for the last twenty-two years. Five years ago he won $50,000.

Bill does not have much formal education, but engages in such creative pursuits as reading, studying history, bird-watching, and painting. Several of his landscapes hang on his walls. We spoke for two hours about history, art, hobbies, and his job. Then, all at once, he concluded:

"You might say that my job gives me a chance to do things I like away from work. But I'm along in my career. If I were thirty, I would tell you something different. But now I'm what you call a loafer. I guess you might say that I'm lazy and unambitious. I like to sleep late and spend time on vacations. It's not that I don't like to work, but things have really changed here. The company is in bad financial shape and they've been laying people off. In three years they have gone from 1,500 workers to 115. There used to be fifteen guys in my section; now I'm the only one. I have to do all kinds of work that my helpers used to do. And I've been putting in long hours to get the work out—forty-five to fifty hours a week. I'm eligible for retirement soon, but I wish they'd lay me off right now. I'm getting out in July, but right now I hate it. Every day I wake up and fight with myself about whether I should go to work.

"There's so much pressure. I make decisions involving hundreds of thousands of dollars. I got high blood pressure because of it. But I love those vacations, and I get twenty days sick leave a year and take them all. We go tramping in a swamp to watch the birds. We really enjoy it, the mud and the water. I wish there was more time to do things like that around here. We're planning to move away from here soon, perhaps to Colorado. We like Maine, too. That's where we usually spend our vacations. We want to get out of this rat race."

It was after ten P.M. We had been talking for two and a half hours. Bill followed me into the hall, closed the door, and began speaking in a low voice:

"You know, I'm a very lucky guy. I believe someone is guiding my life. I was in a very bad car accident a little while ago. A truck forced me off the road. I was doing sixty miles an hour and hit a pole, but I got up and walked away from there and I was only scratched.

"I'm also very lucky with the lottery. I've won many times —$200 once, $50 a couple of times. You know, I've won something in the lottery twenty-seven times. On one stretch I won five out of six weeks.

"The time I won the $50,000, I got a feeling that I should buy the tickets at a special place. I drove ten miles to this store to buy two tickets and one of them won the $50,000. I don't know why I went there—it was out of my way. I never bought tickets there before, but I had this feeling. Another time I had the same feeling and drove into a gas station to buy tickets. I didn't need gas, but I had a feeling that I should go there and buy tickets, and I won $200. I believe in ESP. I think there's something to it, and I'd like to learn more about it."

He lowered his voice another notch, almost whispering:

"You know, things are really changing in this neighborhood. I don't tell anybody about my luck. You don't know what might happen. Burglars have even been around here and broken into several apartments. A car was broken into right outside our apartment. You know, I've got a pistol that I keep under my bed just in case. My wife doesn't like it, but you've got to have some protection these days."

In Bill's story and in most of those that follow, there are common threads, similarities in people's life-styles, jobs, and social integration which provide a key to an explanation of their psychic experiences. Before we attempt to bridge the hiatus between the unknown and reality, let us look into the psychic accounts of other winners. One of the most fascinating was related by Arnold Barker, a forty-nine-year-old shoe salesman.

Arnie, his wife, and their three young children live in a lower-middle-class neighborhood on the outskirts of Buffalo. Their house, an old two-family wooden building with a brick façade, is valued at $28,000. They have lived in it for twenty years.

Arnie seems a bit old to have little children. As he explained it, "We were married eleven years and had none. We were about to adopt when the first one came." It seems that nothing in his life has come easily. For seven years he was a mason, and although the money was good, the working conditions were not. When the opportunity presented itself, he became a salesman. For thirteen years he tried to live on his salary and commissions, but finally was forced to return to masonry as a second job. His financial situation improved, but he was working sixty to seventy hours a week and spending too little time with his family. Then, three years ago, Arnie won $50,000.

When he greeted me at his door, I explained about the study. His first words were, "You can't trust these crooked politicians! They keep you down. Even when you win, they take it away in taxes." He muttered a few more phrases about the manipulation of the "little man."

To avoid paying higher taxes, he had followed the advice of a stockbroker and invested in the market. "I lost $6,000 right away, but I would have lost about the same in taxes if I hadn't invested it. I took the rest out and put it into 'real' investments rather than 'representative' investments."

He would not specify what these "real" investments were

except that they would survive the cataclysmic upheavals he believed the United States and the world would soon be going through. Later he indicated that he had invested about $4,000 in real estate. The rest of the money is in the bank.

It was not only Arnie's lack of faith in the stock market that caused him to lose interest in the economic system. Lately he has been developing an awareness of what he vaguely termed "more important and meaningful investments which can help others." His growing awareness of the unmet needs of his fellow human beings was causing him increasing concern.

"The system is set up to keep you where you are. I think a just society is one where everybody lives and shares together. Where they all work together. I think the greatest satisfaction is to be of service to others. If you're producing, to produce something of quality. If you're in some kind of service, to give good service."

Arnie is not a gambling man. He does not play cards, go to horseraces, or bet on sporting events, so I asked him why he bought the ticket.

As he explained it, in 1971 he enrolled in a one-week course on "mind control." The course costs $150 and is produced by a national organization headquartered in Texas. Arnie believes the skills he learned through this course helped open new vistas of awareness for him; now he could control his physiological and psychological states. "The body is in the mind. The mind is the most important part of us. We must learn to control it and through it our bodies."

Arnie's interest in mind control led him to meet people who dabbled in other parapsychological and occult specialties. Gradually he began to immerse himself in the study of these subjects, particularly ESP and reincarnation, which he firmly believes in. He is also fascinated with the study of past "Masters" of the spiritual world from the East. He frequently spoke of the kahunas of Hawaii, who were believed able to raise the dead. He has also read about and believes in bilocation and astral projection (the processes of projecting one's spirit or inner self into other places), and he vividly described instances involving the practice of these skills by Eastern Masters.

"There was an expedition in Tibet I read about. When the main party was about 150 miles away, one of the Masters lay down and went into a deep trance. As they watched, they could see him become less and less visible until he wasn't there. At that moment the party at the other place saw him."

Arnie is also a religious man, and attends Mass every Sunday. During our conversation he frequently compared the teachings of the Masters with those of the Church and Christ. He also repeated phrases from the Bible which were vaguely analogous to the teaching of the Masters.

Arnie contends that by learning to control our minds, we can commune with the Masters and draw on their infinite wisdom to solve the world's problems. He has become proficient in the art of mind control and practices frequently. He also reads voraciously about occult subjects.

Arnie participates in a group of psychics and mind-control practitioners who use tape recordings and self-hypnosis to improve their physical and mental states. The tapes are $35 each and help you "ventilate your subconscious." To date, nine are available. They are sequential, and one must not listen to them out of order or "grave psychological consequences" might ensue. The tapes were developed locally by a revered physician thought to possess psychic powers, including the ability of astral projection. "He is called the 'healer.' People used to line up outside his door, but he's old now and doesn't practice medicine anymore."

What about mind control? How has it helped you?

"In many ways. I'm able to control my thoughts and my body. I had an ankle swell up on me from listening to the tapes. There's a lot of inner stress you have to go through on them sometimes. They're very involved. I practiced mind control and made the swelling go down. Another member of the group, a woman, had the same problem and she, too, was able to get rid of it that way.

"I learned about using mind control like this from an earlier problem I had. There was a lump on my wrist. I thought it was something I could use mind control on; that it might be related to tension. I tried programming it to disappear. I'd reach my level and concentrate on making it go away. The first time, it went away for about a day. I tried it again and it stayed away for a little longer, but it kept coming back. But the fourth time, it worked for good.

"It was through mind control that I bought the ticket. It was back in March 1972. It was a cold day and I had a lot of problems bothering me, so I went for a walk around the block. There was still snow on the ground and it was cold out. I walked for several blocks and came home feeling a lot better. Then I went into the kitchen and sat down at the table and began to reach my higher level. Suddenly I was overwhelmed by a revelation. It filled me up with a tremendous sense of emotion. It's impossible to describe. It came to me from an all-knowing spiritual awareness, like a sign or impression imprinted on your mind. Like if I said, 'Think of a red Volkswagen,' you can see the picture of it in your mind.

"Words appeared in my mind: 'There will be a great change in your life.' I asked, 'For the good?' and the reply came, 'Yes.' 'How?' and it came back, 'Money.' I said, 'Investments?' and the answer was, 'Lottery.' I asked, 'How many tickets?' and the answer was, 'Three.' 'A month?' and it came back, 'A week.' I never bought lottery tickets before and I didn't know they sold them by the week. I began buying tickets in April. Every once in a while I would reach my level and ask when it was going to happen and the answer would come back, 'Soon.' I did this several times and it happened the night before I won, in July."

That's really something. But why you? Why did the Masters pick you to win the money?

"The Masters were working their way through me. I was only a vehicle for them. Winning the money allowed me to quit my second job and devote more time to reading and practicing mind control. Pretty soon I hope to be able to start teaching mind control to other people. So the Masters were helping me to develop myself and then help others."

Has your life changed since you won?

"There have been a lot of changes in my life since then. I have a greater opportunity to read and practice mind control. My whole attitude about life has changed. My wife has taken the course, too."

Have any of the other people in your group had similar experiences?

"Some have had similar feelings about winning, but they didn't win. One did win $50. Another asked the Masters and was told she would not win."

Do you still buy tickets?

"One a week. For no real reason. Maybe we'll win again, but the need isn't there."

During the interview Arnie had a placid, tranquil expression on his moon-shaped face. He was loquacious and eager to relate his experiences. He firmly believed he had undergone a psychic experience—one which deeply moved him and radically altered his life. Therefore he not only was willing to relate the particulars of this event but did it with enthusiasm in the hope of convincing others of his sincerity.

Several weeks later I described Arnie's experiences during a lecture in one of my sociology classes. I did not use his name, but after class a student told me, "I know the guy you're talking about. I met him at a meeting around here. I practice Zen and he wanted me to teach it to him. He told me the same story."

We know two definite things about Arnie's story: he believes it and he is consistent in describing it. His life provides a clue to the nature of his experience. He actively pursued the study of the occult, and it is conceivable that his readings and practice of mind control enabled him to slip into an ESP experience. Social scientists refer to such a circumstance as a self-fulfilling prophecy: that is, if you define a situation as being real or possible, you may behave so as to make it happen. Arnie believed in the reality of otherworldly spiritual influences on people, and devoted considerable time to an attempt to commune with these psychic forces. It is not unreasonable to assume that his belief in the existence of such phenomena colored his attempt to contact them and precipitated his revelation.* Yet, there is still something missing: what motivated him to study the occult and practice mind control? Let us defer our answer until we review similar experiences.

Advance knowledge of wins sometimes came from friends who told about a feeling or experience which meant that the finalist was going to win. In several cases this foreknowledge was proffered by relatives. Such predictions were not confined to adults, as Robert Whelan, a forty-three-year-old telephone-company supervisor, revealed.

His drawing was on St. Patrick's Day, and, being part Irish, Bob felt that this was a good omen. "I went around telling everybody I was going to win. I went down there with a positive attitude, and that helped me. I don't know what would have happened if I'd lost. I probably would have had a nervous breakdown."

His confidence was bolstered by the behavior of his oldest child, who he believes has some psychic ability. "She was only two at the time, but she kept saying, 'Daddy's gonna win the million.' She didn't even know what it was all about. There were other times, too, like when I would be reading a paper and she would ask me a question about what I was reading—like she already knew, but she didn't even know how to read. She still does this. She does other things, too, like the time I drove down a dead-end street. Just as I saw the sign, she asked why I was going down a dead-end street. She couldn't see the sign or the street because she was too small to see out."

Parapsychologists refer to this phenomenon as precognition, and although there is no conclusive evidence for it, many people have reported similar experiences. The prob-

*Of course, the alternative hypothesis, that Arnie actually had a revelation, is also available.

lem with such phenomena is that they cannot be relied on to predict accurately. We often hear about correct predictions by psychics, but we are seldom reminded of the monumental misses they make in the torrent of prophecies which gushes from them. Still, these events were widespread and intriguing.

While everyone wishes and hopes to win, some contestants tried to influence the outcome of their drawing through psychic manipulation. A few went to unusual lengths. One millionaire reported that she and her fifteen co-workers touched her ticket the day before the finals, and that evening, at a predetermined time, all concentrated in their homes on making her win the next day. Although she believes it helped, she admitted that the technique is not infallible. "They tried it for another woman who was in the finals, but it didn't work."

In a similar vein, another winner revealed one of the secrets which her family believed increased her chances. "It was a bonus drawing. We had to wait ten weeks until the final. The year I won we bought tickets which had the last two numbers '67' at least six times. The winning ticket had this combination, too, and we thought it would bring us luck. When we learned we were in the bonus, we wished we could just win the $7,000 consolation prize. We had to send the ticket in and decided to send in four names—mine, my husband's, and our two children. On the night before the drawing, we got around the kitchen table and held hands, and I said to close our eyes and think hard on winning. We stood there in silence for a few minutes. Then I looked at everyone and said that even if we didn't win, things shouldn't change in the family.

"The day of the drawing my husband came home from work and said we were going to win because his hand itched. Late that afternoon we got a call from the state."

The use of psychic energy to influence the outcome of an event such as a lottery drawing is known as psychokinesis: the movement of objects by mental energy. As with many other parapsychological phenomena, there have been documented cases of persons through whom it works, including a famed Russian woman who reputedly is able to move salt shakers across a table by passing her hands above them. It is conceivable that the psychic energy generated by some people might exceed that of the rest of us, but is it strong enough to stop a rotating roulette wheel on a given number, or to predispose an individual to pick an unnumbered ball containing a specific name which has been revolving in a drum for ten minutes?

Frequently, success was signaled to future winners through a communication from a dead relative or friend. Sometimes this was nothing more than a strange feeling about the presence of a loved one at the time of the drawing —a common experience of widows, as we will see in Chapter 5. Vito Salerno, a forty-two-year-old meat-cutter, won a million dollars three years ago, and recalled the peculiar set of circumstances which led him to buy the ticket that put him in the running for the grand prize.

"It was a funny thing. I woke up one Sunday morning about six. I don't know why, but I couldn't sleep. I never had this problem before, but, for some reason, that morning I got up and I got dressed and went for a ride. That's unusual, too, because I dislike driving. This time I drove to a place where I hadn't been in a long time. We had a dear friend who used to live in the area. He passed away about a year before, and now I found myself back there. I must have been thinking of him, I guess. Anyway, I recognized a store that I knew, and I went in to buy newspapers. On the way out I stopped and bought two tickets. I never bought any before, and my wife didn't even know that I had them. It was odd, wouldn't you say?"

Odd? Strange? Coincidental? Stories such as this proliferated and were accepted as reality by people experiencing them. Minnie Petraglia, a fifty-eight-year-old widow, recounted the following incident:

"I used to buy two lottery tickets a week. That's all I could afford. I got the winning ticket by chance. A friend of mine took me to bingo one night. I like to go, but don't drive, so to thank her for giving me a ride I bought two lottery tickets and gave her one. The other one I kept. That was the one that won.

"The day of the drawing my son and daughter came with me. It was like make-believe. We almost forgot to put our name in the ball. Just before they drew one of the balls, my son said five is the big one. The one that came out next was number five and when they put it up there I knew he was right, but we didn't know our name was in it.

"At about the same time that this was happening my husband's sister, Emily, had a strange experience at work. All of a sudden, she said, she looked up and saw a vision of my husband. He was smiling down at her. She asked him, 'Jimmy, did Minnie win?' She said he just smiled and said, 'Let her tell you.' She said from that moment she knew we won."

Dreams were the medium through which many winners were reportedly contacted by the dead. Often they were told they would win, and sometimes, as with Walter Johnson, there were instructions about how to participate in the drawing.

After serving as a policeman in his town for twelve years, Walter left the force to become a long-haul truckdriver for nine years. He handled big rigs and enjoyed it, even though he worked long hours. His trips took him from coast to coast, and north into the snow belt around Syracuse, New York. He was averaging over $350 a week before he broke his leg in a fall on his back steps.

"Things got pretty tight here before we won. I had a cast on all the way up to my waist. I didn't like to go outside because of it. I just stayed in most of the time. I felt funny, and it was on so long that it began to smell. I received unemployment benefits, but they lasted for only twenty-six weeks. Meanwhile, my son was living with us and going to college.

So was my daughter, and her husband, who was in college, and their baby. My wife was working, but it was impossible to support the whole family on her salary [$7,500 a year]. After I exhausted the benefits—it was in December—I didn't know what to do. Someone suggested that I go to Social Security and get disability."

Mrs. Johnson broke in: "He really hated to go out with that cast on. He went out so seldom that he didn't realize he should have put a sock on over his toes. It was cold out and his toes were turning blue."

"We got into the Social Security office and it was filled," said Walter. "We had to wait a long time, and when we finally saw a man, he said I couldn't get any help. I told him, 'I'm fifty-two and can't work. I've paid into the fund. Don't I qualify for some disability?' He said, 'You couldn't get any if you *lost* your leg, even if you lost both of them!' There I was with my blue toes, looking like a mess and feeling funny. We left.

"I knew something had to be done. I was buying lottery tickets—just two a week. I thought that the only way things would change was if I was going to win. Well, I bought this special ticket for $2.50. One night I was sitting and reading the paper and I happened to see the number for the lottery. I took my ticket out and it looked like it matched all the numbers, but I wasn't sure. I thought maybe I was wrong, so I called my daughter: 'Mary-Jo, come here!' She yelled back, 'What do you want now?' I was in the habit of being waited on a lot and I'd been giving lots of orders, so I guess they were all pretty tired of me. When she came in, she checked it out and I was right.

"This number put us in the finals for the million. You know, the rest is so crazy, I don't know if I should even tell you. I'm a disbeliever in these sorts of things myself. I really hate to get into them because people feel you're wacky. [Long pause.] Well, the night before the drawing, I had this dream. I dreamt I was in a cemetery. I was beside a grave, kneeling down looking into it. There was an open casket in it and my wife's grandfather was inside. He died a year and a half before and we were very close to him. I can still see it. I was standing there looking in and talking to him. All he said was, 'Ralph! Ralph!' That's my son's name. It was all very real, just like it was happening.

"I told my wife about it the next day. I thought he was trying to tell us something. I felt that the only way we were going to win would be through my son. I made up my mind Ralph would do the drawing. Ralph wanted a sports car real bad, but he couldn't afford one. I told him if he went with us and took our place on the stage—you know, taking the ball from the drum—that if we won I'd buy him any one he wanted. He's got a new Triumph now.

"Now, if you sit down and tell people that, they think you're nuts. But I'm smart enough to know that if I had taken that ball out, there's a good chance it wouldn't have been the same one or in the same time and place as for him."

Mrs. Johnson is more of a "believer" than Walter. One of her friends dabbles in the occult: tarot cards, astrology, numerology. On her suggestion, they went to an astrologer shortly after winning.

"She said that the numbers five and eight play an important role in our life. I told her that the winning number had no fives or eights in it, but she wouldn't change her story. When I got home I checked the number on the ticket that got us into the finals and it was 8258.

"I've learned a little about numerology, too. Ever since I can remember, six has been our lucky number. Our son was born on the sixth. Our house number is six and there were sixty-six people in the finals that day. Also, for some unknown reason, before the drawing that day my husband signed the forms Walter instead of Walt, which he always puts. There are six letters in Walter."

Walter was obviously having problems before he won. Aside from the financial crisis precipitated by his broken leg, he was questioning his ability to continue working as a truck-driver. Although winning relieved the financial pressure, it did not solve his ambiguity about returning to driving. Indeed, the money may have intensified his problem.

This was not the case among people who believed their winning was the result of divine intervention. Most of them were deeply religious, hard-working, and habituated to their life's routine. Many viewed their wins as a gift from God— recognition of their good works, perseverance, and fortitude in the face of formidable obstacles such as poverty.

Many of the people attributing religious significance to winning were Catholic. In fact, nearly half the millionaires I interviewed were Catholic—a statistic which might lead an unbaptized gambler to convert. Actually, there are high proportions of Catholics in the states I focused on, and there is a Catholic Church tradition of raffles and bingo.

Winning was not confined to Catholic laity. In upstate New York a few years ago fifteen nuns purchased a ticket and wound up sharing a $100,000 prize. About the same time a young Buffalo priest, Raymond O'Donald, hit for $50,000.

The priest's win was all the more interesting since he rarely purchased tickets.

"My secretary was into it, so I tried. I bought only one a month for seven months. The very first month, I won $100, and I won $50,000 on the seventh try."

Although people knew it was not proper to pray for money, many did, and like Johnnie De Carlo, a New Jersey millionaire, assuaged feelings of guilt and impropriety by using the money in charitable ways.

"About thirty years ago I bought a religious statue from somebody I knew. I didn't have the money to buy it all at once, so I paid him a quarter a week. Many years ago there was a fire in our house and the whole place was destroyed, but the statue was left unharmed. When they were going through the place later on, one of the firemen saw it and couldn't believe it.

"We kept it and felt that it had special power. There are two figures on it. One of them is St. Theresa. I pray to her. The Monsignor said it was wrong to pray to win the lottery.

He was talking about this in church one day, but I did anyway. I prayed to her for the money.

"I pray every day now, and I give a lot of donations to churches. Not just to my church, to all different ones, Protestant, Catholic, Jewish. It was part of my promise when I prayed to win. The first year I gave over $4,000. And I pray to St. Theresa whenever I go upstairs. I get down on my knees and pray to her."

Winning a million dollars might make anyone more religious, especially one who associated the win with prayer. Mrs. Lidia Dubinsky, a widow, didn't win as much as Johnnie, but she firmly believes her winning was part of a divine plan.

She lives with one of her three daughters in an old house in Niagara Falls. I found her chopping ice on the front walk. "I enjoy it. It's my exercise. I used to work as a registered nurse, for over thirty years. First for some doctors in Canada, later at a hospital in Buffalo, and then in private duty. I haven't worked since 1962. I'm seventy years old."

She looks much younger, healthy and vibrant. During our conversation she stressed her positive attitude toward life, good health, the virtues of clean living, and her love of the outdoors. Forty-three years ago she left her native Czechoslovakia and emigrated to Canada, where she lived for eleven years. She married a carpenter and they settled in western New York. Eventually they saved enough money to buy two ten-acre parcels of land from a farmer, and her husband built a house on each.

"There were orchards and gardens. I love the trees and outdoors, but it became too hard to keep up after my husband died. So I sold one of them. The other I leased."

Along with Social Security and some dividends from stocks, this provides the bulk of her modest income, which she shares with people throughout the world. She has a deep love for humanity, especially the poor and oppressed. For over forty years she has been giving generously: clothes, medicine, and money to the needy. Literally hundreds of people receive presents from her throughout the year. "I go

to the post office every day with packages and they ask,
'Where are we going today?'

"I meet many people in churches as I travel. I went to
Europe in 1962 and 1965, from coast to coast. Belgium to
Rumania, every country. At Christmastime I write them all
to pep everybody up. Let them know I'm alive. I send hundreds of cards and I write a little note with every one. The
postage is high, but I don't mind."

She bestowed one of her greatest gifts in 1968 when she
sponsored two Czech families she had befriended on a previous trip, and arranged for them to come to the United States.
"One family had to crawl on their bellies across farmland to
get over the border into Austria." Before they arrived, she
obtained apartments for them and paid their first month's
rent. She filled their refrigerators with food and got jobs for
the men.

Lidia also gives generously to many charities and churches,
regardless of their faith. "As long as they teach from the
Bible. There is only one God. I believe this. I was in Baptist
seminary for two years and I know the Bible from front to
back. When they talk about the Bible and prophecy, I know
what they're talking about. When I listen to them on the
radio or television, I take the phone off the receiver so I'm
not disturbed when they speak."

She has contributed to many evangelists, including Billy
Graham, Rex Humbard, Garner Ted Armstrong, and Oral
Roberts.

"I send money to many of them, but I always check to see
if they are deserving. People are money-hungry. I won't send
to ones that don't need it. I gave $3,000 to churches last year.
A thousand to my church here. Since I've won, more have
benefited."

Her kindness and generosity are appreciated by all who
know her. "I have no enemies. I consider everybody my
friend," and her benevolence has left an indelible mark on
her own family. Although she had twin daughters, shortly
after World War II she took in a young Austrian girl. "She was

starving and in an orphanage. I legally adopted her and brought her here. She is married now and very happy." Lidia has sponsored other children by mail, becoming a surrogate parent, and regularly sends gifts and money for their sustenance.

Her patience, kindness, and nursing skill were helpful in caring for her mother, sister, and husband, who all died of strokes. Her husband was stricken in 1962 and lay near death, paralyzed in a nearby hospital. The doctors offered no hope.

"They told me he had one week to live. I said they were wrong, that I could bring him back. I took him home. They don't care for you there. I wanted him home, near me, so I could take care of him. I slept alongside him on a cot for months. He was being fed through a tube. I massaged his throat. I worked with him. In a little while he was eating regular food. I called the doctor and wanted him to come over and see my husband. He stopped by on his way to the hospital one day. I said, 'See, Doctor? See what I have done?' He couldn't believe it. My husband lived for nearly three years."

Lidia enjoys traveling in the United States as well as abroad. She goes to Florida every year and frequently visits her sister in San Francisco. On the return leg of the San Francisco trip, she routinely stops at Las Vegas to gamble. "She has been there more than twenty times," said Francine, her daughter. "I've been there with her, and she *never* loses."

"I always win enough to pay for the trip and have something left over. I play the slot machines and keno. I enjoy doing it. On a recent trip I was waiting in line to get in somewhere. There was a long line, so I went up to a slot machine and put five nickels in and hit the jackpot. I won $150. I always come back with extra. Then I have some more for bingo. I'm a regular bingo player."

"She never misses a night," said Francine. "She is lucky there, too. She recently won $500."

At a recent church raffle she was late and rushed to get a ticket. No sooner had she bought it than they called out her number. "The same day I won the lottery I played bingo and won twice. Once for $100 and once for $27."

Lidia does not feel gambling is wrong, because she uses the winnings to help other people and "bingo goes to the church to keep up the heat and electricity." Lottery tickets are good because "the money goes for education." Since most of her winnings are distributed to needy people and charities, she believes she is lucky because God is working his way through her. "Many people pray that I help. If you help others, God helps you, God be with you."

She was the first person in her city to win big in the lottery: $54,000. "I had a funny feeling. 'I think I'm going to win the jackpot,' I told my children and, sure enough, I won. When my adopted daughter heard, she said, 'See, Mother? You give slowly and God gave you back in a chunk.'

"I still buy five lottery tickets a week. Right now I have several tickets for the special $250,000 drawing. I hope I hit $250,000. I will, I know it. I can help more people in bigger amounts."

Other people had more selfish, albeit legitimate, motives for beseeching help from the Almighty. Often their prayers were an act of desperation—a last resort. Peter Pulaski found himself in such a situation.

To his fares Peter is the "Singing Cab Driver." As he motors along, he frequently breaks out in one of his ditties. Most are cheerful like the man himself. He is always smiling, and, at fifty-eight, he finally has cause to be cheerful. Life was an uphill battle until three years ago when he won $100,000 in the New York State Lottery. I met him soon after that, when he gave me a ride to the airport. His cab was old and weather-beaten, suffering from "western New York Cancer," a condition characterized by a withering away of the autobody, but he cherished it nevertheless.

"I wasn't always feeling good like this. I struggled all my life. I never had any money. I worked hard in a steel mill as a molder and core-maker for thirteen years, until I got laid off. I'm glad they laid me off, though, or I might still be working there. Sometimes I see some of the guys I knew there. They're ten, fifteen years younger than me and they look old and worn out, like they're old enough to be my grandfather. After that job, I clerked in the A&P, but I couldn't make enough money to make ends meet, so I'd caddy to make extra money. I'd carry three bags at a time. Then I began driving a cab. I was broke before I won the money. I owed the bank $4,000 and they were about to foreclose on my mortgage. Things were so bad I even bought some vegetable seeds and planted them in the backyard. We were just eating lettuce-and-tomato sandwiches. I was really desperate.

"You know, you're not supposed to pray for money in the Catholic Church. They bring you up that way. You can pray for others, for health. . . . I was in such bad shape, though, that I went to church and prayed for money. It was a personal thing. I was there in the chapel and I told God that I realized it wasn't right to pray for money, but I really needed it. After all, He put us here and you need money to live. I asked for $5,000. I lit three candles and I signed the paper which asks what your intentions are: 'To win the lottery.' A few days later I found a dollar by the curb, and later that day I found a pencil outside Loblaw's [supermarket]. I went in and used the dollar to buy a lottery ticket and filled out the form with the pencil I found. You know, a guy offered me $100 for that pencil. After I won, I went back to church and thanked God, but I said, 'You kind of overestimated my need.' "

Some people engaged in ritual prayers called novenas. These are lengthy, strung over nine days, but Celeste Borkowski developed an abbreviated version which she claims is highly successful.

The Borkowskis and their son, Bob, won $50,000 two years ago. They live in a Polish enclave in the center of Buffalo, where the streets are narrow and the houses neat and well kept. The porches of many homes are decorated with ornate wrought iron that varies the army-barracks appearance of the neighborhood. Their home is 130 years old. Celeste's parents gave it to her, and after winning, she gave it to Bob. The inside was a shambles because extensive remodeling was being done to convert the two downstairs rooms into three. Celeste was elated about this: "I always wanted three rooms. This was my dream as a little girl."

At forty-six, Celeste is cheerful and energetic, the matriarch of the home. Prior to winning, she held two jobs—as a part-time clerk in a supermarket and a full-time laborer in a factory. Some weeks she worked thirteen hours a day, six days a week, and she averaged less than $5,000 a year. After they won, she quit the supermarket job. "Before, I had to work as much as I could, there was no other way." They were in dire financial straits, frequently running out of money. "That was the main topic here," she said. They owed many bills, but the most disturbing one was a $150 deficit in their son's tuition at a nearby Catholic college.

Bob is their only child, and they sacrificed to get him things they'd never had. They bought him a used Corvette, and worked hard to put him through college so he could have more than his father, who had only an eighth-grade education. But in the end, even with all three of them working, they could not manage, and Bob had to drop out a year and a half before graduation. Celeste, a devout Catholic, turned to God for help.

"I'm not a religious nut, but I do believe in the Infant of Prague, so I made a novena. I didn't ask for money, just for guidance so maybe I'd be put on the right way. It normally takes nine days, but I do it in nine hours. I finished on Wednesday. On Thursday I met my husband coming home [they work different shifts, he in the day and she at night] and he had tears coming down his face. I thought something had happened to Bob. I asked him what was the matter and he said, 'I think I hit the lottery.' I said, 'Great!' figuring he had won $50 like he did the week before. 'That's $50 less, now I only need $100 more for

Bob's tuition.' He said, 'No! I think I won the $50,000!'

"I have only made two other novenas, and each time it's worked. The first time was when my husband was sick. It was in 1955. He had bleeding ulcers and only worked three days a week. Bob was sick too and I was laid off. I kept trying to find a job, but couldn't. I went to Trico's and kept filling out employment applications—fifteen of them. I was ready to give up, and then I made a novena to the Infant of Prague. I finished it at nine o'clock, and at nine fifteen I got a telegram from them to come and get my job.

"The second time was when my son wanted to go to college in the day. He wanted to switch from nights, but a young priest who was in charge was giving him trouble. He wanted him to wait a year before he could go back. I talked with him, but he wouldn't give in, so I made a novena to the Infant of Prague. A couple of weeks later I was painting a room in the house and the name of a priest came to me. He was respected in the area, and so I made an appointment with him about the matter. He called the other priest, but he still wouldn't give in. Then this priest went to see the college priest and they took my son in right away. I didn't know this priest personally. We aren't even in his parish. Now, what prompted me to think of him?"

And what of the son they labored so hard for? Bob, now twenty-six, graduated from college last year, worked for a few months as an insurance salesman, but did not like it. Celeste then got him a laborer's job at her plant.

Some people were so convinced their winning was divinely ordained that they used the opportunity to offer a testimony to God. With evangelical zeal, Ronald Carlson, a thirty-three-year-old railroad brakeman, harangued the crowd at his drawing and launched into a discourse about the virtues of accepting Christ in your life. Lottery officials were dumbfounded when he belittled the importance of his million-dollar windfall.

"We're Christians. Winning the lottery was the second most important thing in our lives. The first most important thing was when we accepted Christ. It happened to me on March 29, 1972. That day I confessed to God and admitted Christ into my life. I think gambling is wrong—my wife never approved of me buying the tickets. I prayed for the Lord's will in my life. I didn't pray to win, but to have the Lord's testimony in my life.

"I bought the tickets for three months to win $10,000 to buy a new home. It wasn't real gambling which takes money from the family. I didn't feel guilty about it, but I didn't tell anyone about it either. I viewed it as a testimony. *He* willed it. The Lord wouldn't give it to you if you couldn't take care of it. God is in your life if you are with Him. If you're in the faith, God is in you and your life, and He'll answer your prayers."

The Carlsons say they eschew worldly possessions. Unlike other winners, they have not bought a new car. Lora Carlson still drives a 1966 Chevrolet, and Ron drives a 1968 Dodge pickup.

"The money made my sons very happy, though," said Ron. "They had been asking for minibikes, but I was unable to buy them. That night when we got home we found a note from my oldest boy: 'Dear Dad, I know you can afford it now. Are you going to have enough left to buy me a Honda minibike?'

"I told a reporter that I was going to give some money to charity. Then I got a call from a college. They asked me to give them $10,000 so they could buy books for their library. I suppose that they had a good cause, but I wanted to give my money to the church."

In appreciation for what they believe God has done for them, the Carlsons voluntarily tithe their annual lottery check, giving their church ten percent. Ron explained: "The church puts the money in the bank and gets savings certificates. They're going to use it to expand the sanctuary."

Lora Carlson, thirty-one, is also devoutly religious, having been recently converted to the faith. She sprinkles her conversation with verses from the Bible. Born in Germany of Polish parents, she came to the United States twenty-three years ago. She recalled what it was like in Germany after the war: "We used to hope and pray to come to this country. We used to sing 'The Star-Spangled Banner'. "

Ron works from four P.M. to midnight as a brakeman for the Penn Central Railroad. "If you have a job you enjoy, why give it up? Especially at my age. I enjoy working outside. I worked in a factory and didn't like it. I might retire at forty-five—I don't know. But I think it's important to keep busy and active in your community. You feel like you're accomplishing something. You have to work to be a help to society. Why be a bum?"

We were standing at a railroad crossing now and it was dusk. There were no protective gates, lights, or bells to warn motorists, so Ron lit several flares to signal cars and the engineer driving the locomotive. Cars were zipping past us as we stood on the tracks listening for the telltale crunch ahead which signaled that an empty boxcar would be propelled in our direction. It was difficult to see in the growing darkness, and the air was chilled by a brisk wind which made our hands ache inside our gloves. I turned to him and asked how long he planned to keep this job.

"Well, for the time being, I'm satisfied, but I'm thinking about going into real estate. I'd like to take a real-estate course and get my license. I may leave here in two years, then I'll be able to freeze my pension. One reason I didn't quit was because of the benefits. I get free health insurance, too, but I was happy before, because we knew Christ was our Saviour. Worldly goods don't bother us. You come into this world without anything—without any material possessions— and that's the way you're going to leave. If I had to choose between money and Christ, I'd give the money back."

Similarities among the winners provide us with insights into the possible causes for their supernatural experiences. Most significant among the shared characteristics of these people is their low income level, averaging under $10,000 before taxes prior to winning. The lottery catapulted them out of poverty into affluence. This abrupt change in their social and economic status may have been a traumatic shock. The stories could have evolved as a method of rationalizing this disruptive event.

As we noted, some people, especially those having religiously oriented experiences, viewed winning as a gift from God—a reward for their piety. It is conceivable that many winners believed they were among the chosen few who deserved to win. The odds against winning were so high, twenty or thirty million to one, and yet *they* won or, as some obviously preferred to believe, were *selected* to win. Winning, in such cases, may be interpreted as a sign of divine recognition of their virtues. This belief resembles the Puritan concept of the "elect," a doctrine which held that only certain people would be allowed to join God in heaven.

Many successful people in our society point with pride to their accomplishments in work, but few winners had occupations in which they could demonstrate their merit. In winning, and in their subsequent interpretations of spiritual and divine intervention, they were able to point to their worthiness, justifying and rationalizing the incredible event which befell them.

Another common characteristic of winners was their low educational level; none had graduated from college. Lacking knowledge about science and an intellectual grasp of society and the world, they may have turned to religion and the quasi-scientific realm of parapsychology for explanations and interpretations of their winning and experiences. While science can provide answers about the empirical, tangible events which shape our lives, religion and the occult proffer answers about the unknown. Though we may be skeptical, one cannot emphatically disprove the existence of a spiritual world. Since many winners had prior knowledge of ESP and many were deeply religious, it could be expected they would draw on these areas for explanations. Furthermore, it is likely some psychic and religious experiences were even precipitated by people whose strong belief created the experiences for them. This manufacturing of events—what was earlier referred to as a self-fulfilling prophecy—probably occurred quite unconsciously and seemed very real. Through subsequent discussions and elaborations the experiences may have become embellished and more concretized, extinguishing lingering doubts about their authenticity.

Heavy taxation of winnings was another problem shared by winners. Since they had relatively low earnings and taxes before winning, they were appalled by the huge bite which the IRS took. Promised a certain amount, they received a third to a half less. Concomitant with this dismaying realization was the often routine auditing of their returns and other reported harassment by the IRS (see Chapter 6). In addition, many people had other negative experiences. They were harassed by friends, neighbors, family; subjected to badgering by aspiring investors, con artists, and charities; under constant pressure from the moment they won. They resented being exploited, having to endure the psychological pain and the loss of privacy the money brought. To insulate themselves from the avaricious, they moved, frequently becoming social isolates. Yet, they were incapable of stopping the harassment by the curious and selfish who wanted to "steal" their gifts. Many people were disgusted and appalled by these intrusions, and deeply resented a federal administration which at the time was itself involved in tax fraud and conspiracy. The real rub was that most of them had voted for President Nixon. The lying and conspiracy of Watergate were bad, but the most devastating blow to them was learning that the President had paid little income tax while *they* were forced to return much of their winnings.

The dreams were turning into nightmares. The blessing was threatening to turn life into a living hell. Powerless to influence the political process and restore equity through actions in the "real" world, some people turned to the supernatural in an attempt to explain and direct their lives, which were becoming increasingly confused and meaningless.

Even though a large proportion of winners reported having such experiences, numbers alone do not prove that psychic or religious forces influence a person's winning. To demonstrate cause and effect between such events and their outcomes would require rigorous experimentation, the absence of which makes the experiences simultaneously scientifically unacceptable and provocative. The methodological tools of science are presently unable (and they may never be able) to measure such non-empirical phenomena as angels or paracletes. Scientists can, however, study such sociological phenomena as the shared characteristics of people who have undergone such experiences, in an attempt to find a clue to the causes of their behavior in the empirical world. This is what has been attempted on these pages. In the final analysis, unless one is a "true believer," the individual stories must remain what they were reported to be—extraordinarily intriguing accounts.

CHAPTER 3

Fortune's Reckoning: Harassment and Fear

"No doubt you have lots of requests for donations
and I am making another one."
—*From a letter received by a lottery winner*

They came to the drawings in search of the good life, to
exchange harried old lives for tranquil new ones. They believed winning would launch them into idyllic dream
worlds free of financial worries, onerous jobs, tension, and
insecurity. Instead, they found they had swapped one set of
problems for another. The instant fame and fortune promised in the glossy lottery ads said nothing about the endless phone calls from well-wishers and pranksters; the
countless letters from strangers; and the threats, intimida-
tion, harassment, loss of privacy, and broken relationships
with family and friends which often accompany such celebrity status.

This is the unexpected side of the life of wealth they aspired to, and many winners were unprepared and unable to
cope with these nightmarish intrusions into their lives and
dreams. The transition to a new life-style is not easy in the
best of circumstances, and the harassment these people were
subjected to frequently disoriented them. It served notice
that things would never be as private and sedate as before.

Now they were newsworthy objects of public scrutiny, their good fortune a matter of record for the needy to beg of and the avaricious to prey upon. They seemed the target of crackpots, cons, and crooks around the world.

From the moment they won, they were subjected to numerous interviews. It was not unusual to find reporters around their homes, at their places of business, or their children's schools. In some cases their friends and neighbors were questioned about their habits and life-styles. The pressure was so intense that some winners stayed away from their jobs to avoid reporters. Public interest in them usually lasted a few weeks, until a new winner was announced, but, periodically inquisitive newsmen would interview previous winners and this would invariably trigger a spate of new calls and letters.

In the beginning, winners were not hostile toward the media. Some even enjoyed their celebrity status. Their initial friendly reaction stemmed from more than egotistical motives. Many were grateful to the state for providing them a secure future and consented to interviews out of a sense of obligation to the lottery commission, "to help them out." This attitude frequently faded, however, when the publicity precipitated a barrage of calls and mail, or when the stories were grossly distorted. One millionaire told me:

"If you were a reporter, you wouldn't be sitting in that chair now. One of them came over here one day to interview me. I was hesitant about talking to him, but I let him in. He sat in that chair where you are now and we talked for over half an hour. He wrote down about half a page of notes and the next day his paper ran a story on me that was a column and a half long. There was hardly a word I said there; most of it he just made up."

Two others described the humiliation their wives experienced after being interviewed by female reporters. The women were described as poor housekeepers having dirty unattractive houses. "This really hurt my wife," said one irate husband. "She had just decorated the house and it cost us a fortune. She was really proud of it and was very upset."

Blanche and Chester Gordon, who live in a small town in southern New Jersey, experienced a variety of problems. She is fifty-two and he fifty-five. Their small white ranch house stands out incongruously among similar modest but well-kept homes on their quiet street because it is ringed by a high chain-link fence. On a huge oak tree in the front, to the right of the driveway, hangs a sign, "BEWARE OF DOG." The fence and sign are new, added in response to the turbulence which shattered the serenity of their lives three years ago, after they won a million dollars.

I approached the house with some trepidation and gingerly knocked on the locked screen door. Chester unbolted the inner door, walked across the porch, and peered down at me.

"I've had too many problems," he said in response to my request for an interview. "I'm afraid to speak any more about it. You wouldn't believe the stories I could tell you."

But he relaxed as we chatted through the screen, and in a few minutes invited me into the living room. A toy poodle jumped on my lap and began licking my hand.

Is this the dog the sign warns about?

"Yes," he said sheepishly. "You'd be surprised how many people see that sign and stay away. But, still, we had our share of problems.

"There were threats. My brother got a call. They thought he was me. They said, 'We know who you are and we're going to get a chunk.' I've got my suspicions about who they were. Colored guys from the other part of town. Another time I found two guys out front of the house. I went out to take a closer look. They were bruisers, great big guys. They could have torn me apart. They were standing across the street and looking the house over. I could hear them mumbling to each other. I went inside and then decided to get another look, so I went out the side entrance. They were still there. I got in my car in the driveway, turned it around, and shined the high beams on them. They jumped in their car and drove away.

"Another time we were in the supermarket and as I left I

noticed a man was following us. I went back so as not to leave my wife alone and I noticed he was still hanging around. When we were ready to check out, he came up and said, 'Unemployment's lousy.'

"There were other annoyances. The phone kept ringing. It was so bad we didn't eat for three weeks. We didn't even have time to go outside to shop. All we had was sandwiches. I told my daughter one day, 'If that phone rings again, I'll tear it off the wall.' Just as I said 'wall' it rang. I called the operator and said, 'I have a problem.' She asked me what it was and I said, 'One damn million's worth.' She must have thought I was drunk. Then I explained what I meant and a few days later they changed our number.

"Well, my wife finally got to the supermarket and bought us a big steak. While she was gone a friend of mine came over with his five kids. We couldn't even eat the steak. We had to have sandwiches again!

"People drove up and would sit out there and point at our house. We'd go to the supermarket and people wouldn't leave you alone. One day the cashier looked at us and said, 'No use asking you how you're doing.' You felt like you were under somebody's foot. It's like with these friends of ours. They have a nice pool and always invite us to use it, but we never do. I never wanted to use them or take advantage of their generosity. Now I know how they feel. You don't know if people are coming to see you or to use you.

"I got all sorts of people offering me investments. One guy wanted me to invest in an apartment house. It seemed like a good idea until I found out he wanted me to do all the maintenance. I told him he was crazy if he thought I'd get up at three in the morning to fix someone's faucet. There was one deal that seemed pretty good. The guy said I could get eighteen percent interest the first year if I invested in his business. I asked my lawyer about it and he said to stay away. One fellow, a judge, passed the word that if I retained him for $1,500 a year I'd never have to pay any taxes. I think he appeals all the rulings. I didn't do it.

"I even got a letter from a guy who wanted me to buy him a bus for his drum-and-bugle corps. He said he'd bring them to town and play the national anthem for me! One day an old friend of mine came by. I hadn't seen him for years. He asked for $500. I told him my money was all tied up at the time. He went away and came back two weeks later. This time he asked me for $5,000. I said if I couldn't give him $500, how was I going to give him ten times as much? He got angry. You know what he said? 'Whata you want? Even if I never gave it back, you'll never miss it. It only cost you fifty cents for the ticket.' I never saw him again.

"There were even troubles in the family. There was some jealousy. They think you're gonna help them more. They tell you how you should spend it: 'I'd have a big house,' or 'I'd have a yacht.' They think you can give it away and just take it off your taxes."

The types of problems the Gordons were experiencing plagued most lottery winners. Early winners bore the brunt of the harassment because they received more publicity. Fences and dogs could not keep people away. They came to hurl insults, to hawk wares, or to inveigle the new millionaires into one scheme or another. Once, while I was speaking with a millionaire on his porch about the problem of harassment, a man drove by, honked the horn, waved, and gave him a big smile. The winner looked at me with disgust. "He's one of them. He wants me to buy municipal bonds." Some fortune hunters employed more sinister tactics, such as burglaries of winners' residences. These usually took place shortly after they won. "It was," as one elderly victim put it, "like they think you must have the money just lying around the house waiting for them to come and pick it up."

Not everyone perceived the irritations as severe problems. A few people were quite cavalier about winning and did not appear to be bothered by the publicity or its aftermath. Two people displayed their winning certificates in their places of business. A few others reveled in the attention they received and regularly consented to interviews for the media. Such openness, however, was rare.

In contrast to this extroverted life-style was the far more common defensive, apprehensive reaction. Many winners had placid, sheltered lives prior to winning, and the magnitude of this event heightened their suspicions about people's intentions and pushed them further into introverted lifestyles. Even the more relaxed winners were never free of the fear that their families might be the targets of a malicious act. Something happened one evening at the home of one of the more outgoing millionaires which illustrates this undercurrent of fear. It was 6:30. Supper was ready, but his seven-year-old daughter was not present. The doorbell rang, and when he opened the door nobody was there. Immediately, calls for the little girl echoed throughout the house and the family was mobilized. The grandmother manned the phone, and an older child was dispatched to search the neighborhood. After a few minutes the child was located at a friend's house. Despite the openness and nonchalance the family displayed, this somewhat commonplace incident was handled with the utmost gravity and immediately created a state of mild hysteria.

Two winners hinted that attempts had been made to extort money from them. Information about this is sketchy, since the subject is taboo among winners because they fear publicity might precipitate more threats. Several people did, however, express the fear that their children might be kidnapped. One advised me to use a pseudonym in this book because "You know who we are and where we live. They might try to get at us through you."*

Winning touched their personal lives in many ways. Old friends sometimes reacted strangely toward them, perhaps because they recognized the sudden disparity in their eco-

---

*Although this research has received a great deal of publicity, I have not been the object of such action. I did, however, receive an inquiry from a man who wanted to know if I knew any winners who might consider "serving mankind by giving 70 to 100 percent of their winnings away."

nomic statuses. More often friendships were broken because of jealousy. As one middle-aged widow recalled, "I had friends who wouldn't talk to me anymore. People I knew all my life. They stayed away from me like I had the plague or something. But I didn't let it bother me. If that's the way they felt, then it was their problem."

Passing acquaintances suddenly appeared asking for loans. Some who would not deign to say hello before, now fawned over the instant celebrities. One Pennsylvania millionaire was invited to join a businessmen's association which previously had refused to admit him. Another millionaire related the following incident:

"The day before the drawing, I was putting in a bathtub for this woman. She said she was a poverty nun. She lived in a furnished room. The place was a mess. There was no bathtub, no place to wash. Boy, she was a weird one! Every week she'd get a brush and go across the street and polish a bronze statue. I told her I wouldn't be there tomorrow because I had to go to the lottery and win a million dollars. I never went back. She started sending letters asking me to come back and finish. She even drew pictures of bathtubs on the envelopes. Then she called and asked for $500. I told my wife to write her out a check for $100.

"We even went out shortly after that and bought her some gifts. One was a statuette of the Virgin Mary. We went up to her apartment and she wasn't there, so we left them for her. A few days later she called up and spoke with my wife. She said she called to thank me for the gifts and then she asked, 'Is your husband still buying tickets?' My wife said I was and then she said, 'Well, I hope and pray to God that he never wins again.' "

Relations with co-workers can become strained after winning even a small amount. A sentiment often arose in the place of employment that a winner no longer needed to work and was depriving someone else of a job. Most winners were convinced that the real cause of the friction was jealousy. Supervisors had difficulty relating to workers who were suddenly catapulted into an economic bracket above their own. Some people anticipated on-the-job harassment and never returned after winning. Others, as we will see in Chapter 4, were forced to quit because the pressures became too intense.

Most painful of all were the frictions which sometimes developed among family members because of jealousy or envy. Serious breaks occurred between husbands and wives, parents and children, siblings, and in-laws who harbored expectations about shares they did not receive. Because the wounds were deep, winners were reluctant to discuss such conflict, but several families were figuratively torn apart in the scramble for the money, and they have remained that way. The acrimony lingers on. Even fathers and sons have parted over the money. During a conversation with a $100,000 winner in New York, the following exchange occurred:

"You said you had two sons. How did they react to your winning?"

"Shhh. Not so loud. My older son is upstairs. He lives in the apartment up there, but he's getting ready to move out and go back to the Midwest. He's mad at me. He wanted me to give him $20,000 to buy a new house, and I gave him $1,000. So now he's moving out. I worked hard all my life to support my family. He never helped that much when *I* needed it."

There might well have been no love lost between these two before the win, but, as in a number of other cases, the tension precipitated by it exacerbated nascent conflicts. However, breaks occurred in some solid, close relationships, such as the one between a thirty-year-old millionaire and his cousin.

"I actually got my job through my cousin. He worked at the plant and told me about it. We were very close. He helped me qualify for the job and trained me for several weeks. I'm very grateful for this—how much he will never know.

"The problems with my cousin started in a funny way. Three and a half weeks before I won, I knew I was in the finals. I was at his house and we were sitting in the kitchen around a table. I was joking around and said to him, 'You know what I'm going to do if I win? I'm gonna get you a new car. As a matter of fact, I'm gonna get you a Fleetwood Brougham—fully loaded with all the extras.' Just as I said this, his brother and father walked in and I said to them with a wave of my arm, 'And I'm gonna get you one and you one, too.' I was only kidding. I was exhausted at the time, from working ten hours a day and commuting four.

"Well, I won and took off a week from work. That Sunday, at the christening of my sister's first child, my cousin was there and there seemed to be something between us. He seemed to be brief—not hostile, but brief about things. I didn't know what was the matter. When I went in to work the next week, someone asked me, 'Are you gonna get them the cars?' I didn't know what he was talking about. I had forgotten the whole thing. My cousin was really cool at work. Man, he was cool. He acted like I had the plague. I packed my stuff and I bid my goodbyes to the higher-ups. Then I walked over to my cousin's boss and he said to me, 'Are you going to get him a car?' 'Get who a car?' I asked. 'Your cousin,' he said. 'Are you kidding me?' I left with no recollection of what I had originally said.

"About ten weeks later—it was two and a half months after I won—I stopped up at my cousin's house. I told him I was coming and I wanted to talk with him. I had bought a new Dodge station wagon and drove it there that night. I asked him if he wanted to come with me for a ride. I wanted to be alone with him so I could get down to the bottom of the problem that I wasn't sure was there. I told him for the first hour how great things were going for me. Then for ten minutes nothing was said. There was total silence. Then I said to him, 'What is bugging you? What is it?' He turned to me and asked, 'What about the new car you were gonna get me?' I hesitated and said with disbelief that I was only kidding about that. I had no idea I had even said this. I didn't know what he was talking about. Then he goes, 'Oh, yeah?' For the next thirty-five minutes not a word was said. I tried to start a conversation, but it just fell flat.

"I told my family I didn't understand what the problem was. He never returned my phone calls. I never heard from him again, and we were like brothers."

Bickering over winnings even destroyed marriages. A Pennsylvania State Lottery official related the story of one couple who split up. The husband checked his ticket for the weekly winning number and, seeing it did not match, threw it in the wastebasket. His wife came across it and noticed that a second number on it qualified for the million-dollar-bonus drawing. Without telling him, she attended the drawing, captured the grand prize, took off for Florida, where she currently resides, and filed for divorce. At last notice, her irate ex-husband was suing for half the money. A precedent has been set in two similar cases. In Maryland, a judge ruled that a million-dollar winner must split his remaining installments with his former wife, and in New Jersey, Myron Lasser, a thirty-six-year-old accountant, was on the losing end of a similar decision. He contends that winning $200,000 precipitated his divorce. I found him at his suburban split-level home one Saturday morning with his second wife, Cathy, who was expecting their first child. We discussed the circumstances which led to his break-up.

"I bought the ticket, to begin with. When we won, I had both names on the thing and then someone from the lottery told me that I could only have one name on it,* so I took hers off. I meant nothing by this, but when she found out, she got mad and that's when the battle royal began. It didn't stop until we split up, and even then it continued. We fought and fought over whose money it was. The state didn't know what the hell to do. Then we started getting a divorce. It was a messy thing, with her mother giving me a hard time. I could see then that the only people who would make money on the

---

*This information was incorrect. State regulations concerning the number of payees' names on a winning ticket vary, but multiple names are often accepted.

deal were the lawyers. The judge awarded her thirty-six percent as part of the divorce settlement. That leaves me with
sixty-four percent. It sounds like a lot, but we get only $20,-
000 a year for ten years and that means that I get $12,500 a
year. After taxes I'm left with only $8,000—not much to show
for a $200,000 win, is it?"

In all probability, these marriages were already in trouble
before the win. Actually, most marriages were salubriously
affected by it. With financial worries behind them, many
people manifest a brighter outlook on life. There is less nag-
ging and haggling between spouses and more time and
money to share with one another. As the wife of a forty-two-
year-old millionaire who quit his job explained: "People ask
me how I stand him being here all day. At first I wasn't sure
how it would work out, but now I like it. He helps out with
the kids and does the shopping for me. He helps with the
cleaning around the house and with the gardening. I think
we can share more things now than before."

Some winners simply refused to allow the money to interfere with their lives. One big-spending millionaire looked at
it this way:

"I've been hooked for thousands, but it's in the family."

Some stories have humorous aspects, such as this one
related by the wife of a Pennsylvania millionaire. When
asked if the money had created any strains in her family, she
paused and began:

"Well, I don't think I should say anything, but I might as
well tell you. One of my husband's sisters buys tickets for us
from Pennsylvania. She sells them to the whole family regularly. One of the tickets she sold my husband was the winner.
The day of the drawing we were at the finals together, then
we separated for a while. Right after my husband won, I was
walking by a group of people and I saw my sister-in-law in
the middle. She was being interviewed by some reporters
and I overheard her say she was the sister of the man who
won and that my husband was going to give her ten percent.
Well, I put her right in her place! He never promised any

such thing. Anyway, the ticket she sold him only got him into the finals. That was only worth $600. Then he had to turn it in along with 150 other $600 winners and he got a new ticket which then won him the million. So she really didn't sell him the winner."

Did he give her the ten percent?

"No, he's giving her $10,000 gradually, but she still wants $100,000."

Although they no longer speak, her sister-in-law still sells them tickets—but from a distance. Each week she drives up to their mailbox, which stands on the street in front of their house, inserts several tickets, and removes the money left for her.

Aside from fractured personal relations, other discomfiting annoyances accompanied winning. Phone calls were particularly irksome, often beginning within minutes after the winners were announced. It was not unusual for unsuspecting family members to be deluged with calls before the winner got home. For days afterward, the phone would ring incessantly from five or six in the morning to two or three the next morning—until the harried winner would have it disconnected or the number changed. The Gordons, being among the more obstinate winners, stuck it out for three weeks before throwing in the towel. Today, all but a few winners have unlisted numbers.

Actually, most calls were congratulatory, but some were obscene, and there were threats, pleas for money, and solicitations. Several winners got calls from quarrelsome, intoxicated people who berated them for winning: "Why did *you* win and not me? You don't deserve it. I should have the money because I need it more than you."

The greatest number of solicitations came from stockbrokers and insurance salesmen, but many strangers asked for money, too. One millionaire recalled: "The first call I got was from a guy in town: 'I don't know why you won. I need the money more. I need an operation and I should have won.' I told him, 'Well, sir, I need the money, too. My brother is having an eye operation and I'm going to help him.' "

Another millionaire recounted the following incidents. "An old lady from the Bronx called me and asked if I would give her money so she could take a trip to Ireland. I had no idea who she was. Then I got a call from this guy who was trying to sell his dry-cleaning business. It was sort of funny. He gave me this big spiel and when he was through, I said, 'Listen, if you read the paper you know I'm fifty-seven and about to retire. What makes you think that I want to get involved in such a business now?' Well, he started to agree with me and wound up confessing that his business was really bad. At the end he even thanked me for listening to him."

In one instance the phone was used in an attempt to con a winner out of prize money. "We knew we were in the finals that day for the big prize, but the drawing was held in Albany and we couldn't go. All day I waited for some news, and then, late in the afternoon, we got a call from a man. He told us we won the big prize and he was the one who spun the wheel which landed on our number. He said he was sick and needed $1,000 for doctors' bills and wouldn't it be nice if we gave it to him to show him our gratitude.

"I didn't know if he was telling me the truth, and his story was suspicious, so I called the local representative of the lottery in Buffalo. He told me that he hadn't received any word yet about the winner and he'd call me as soon as he did. I waited for another hour and called him back. This time he seemed irritated and said that he still hadn't heard anything. Just then he said something was coming over the ticker tape and told me to hang on. He came back and said, 'Say, what did you say your name was again?' Then I told him about the call we got and he said by no means should we give the man anything. He put me in contact with the FBI, and the FBI told us they already knew who the man was. He attends the drawings and then tries this on winners."

The winners were also inundated with letters. Many bore the good wishes of friends and relatives, but the mail was laden with solicitations from strangers seeking gifts, loans,

advice, or cajoling, even threatening. Some winners had am-
bivalent feelings about these communications. While they
were constantly reminded of their accessibility and vulnera-
bility, they also recalled their own earlier struggling lives,
and empathized with the people who wrote of their poverty,
lack of education, illness, and desperation. Some letters were
humorous, but most were heart-rending, written by pathetic
outcasts, forgotten people, invisible in their misery. On the
following pages are some letters received by winners. Only
the names have been changed to protect the anonymity of
the senders and receivers.

The letters often revealed the multiple problems of the
poor. Failing health and inadequate medical care were
prominent reasons for beseeching aid. For example, "I know
you think I am crazy But would you help a Black family go
back south. I am not able to work any more, I keep falling
Down and broke my hip."

A letter from an elderly widow asked a millionaire for
money for her paralyzed sister: "She is really a problem to
care for and belongs in a nursing home but we can't afford
to get her in a good one. I pray that you can make a contribu-
tion to her nursing care."

The letters, frequently written in garbled English, are
poignant. They were a last resort, a search for a glimmer of
hope. Begging is beyond the pale of accepted avenues of
assistance in our society, and the writers recognized this,
acknowledging that their petitions were unusual and insist-
ing they were not "crazy." They vividly depicted their
needs. The money was not really for themselves, but for
someone else—a sick brother, an ailing wife, a dying mother,
or a child. Writers often paid homage to the Protestant work
ethic by asserting their belief in self-reliance; hence many
requests were couched in terms of loans to be repaid after
the money was used industriously. They argued that wealth
had been given to the winner (there were frequent refer-
ences to the beneficence of God), who should grant them
seed money so they could break out of their poverty. Estab-

lishing consciousness of kind—that is, linking the prior lives of winners with their own—was common, and their petition was made more appealing by embracing the virtues of thrift and individual initiative in their plans for utilizing the money.

To further persuade winners of their sincerity, they offered to pay interest on the loans, although at a lower, "fairer" rate than banks received. If their stories were true, they not only needed the money but in all likelihood could not have qualified for loans from legitimate lending institutions. They were frequently unemployed, in debt, and had few assets. Some writers went to great pains to paint a dismal picture of their lives. They laid out their income, spending, debts, and household expenses in an impassioned attempt to convince the winners of the dire straits they were in, but to no avail, for most winners ignored them. A $100,000 winner in western New York showed me a handwritten twenty-six-page plea which meticulously outlined the desperate economic situation of a laborer in a meat-packing plant in New Hampshire. He earned $125 a week, but could not support his wife and five children. They owed thousands of dollars and were asking for a $5,000 loan. To convince the winner of his honesty, he vowed, "I'll even come down to see you and show you the bills. You say the word and I'll be there, standing on your front porch. Just let me know and I'll take the next train down." As he read these lines to me, the already skeptical winner blurted out, "That's all I need."

Many writers were having financial problems from overextending themselves, but occasionally a winner might receive a letter like the following one, written by a sixty-five-year-old widow telling how her money had been in a bank that she thought was "Government Protected," but was now in the hands of a receiver. She was on the verge of losing her life's savings and asked the winner to "help me pray they pay me."

Many writers were elderly and implored winners to come to their aid. They sought advice, counseling, and prayers. They asked for gifts, loans, bequests, and understanding.

Often begging and pleading, these forlorn, forgotten Americans laid bare their personal tragedies. They complained of having no house, no clothes, no car, no food, no teeth, no legs, no freedom, and, above all, no money. Money was the universal medium through which their needs could be met, and they dared to beg the newly rich for it. Their advanced age precipitated health problems, and there were frequent requests for cash to pay medical bills and obtain prosthetic devices. Eyeglasses and artificial limbs were commonly desired. One winner received a letter from a ninety-year-old man in the Bronx, written in barely legible Italian.

"I took the letter to work and asked one of the women I work with to translate it for me. It was very complimentary. He congratulated me for winning all the money and said that I looked very nice and friendly from my picture in the paper. Two days later I got another letter from him. This time he got right to the point. He said that since I had all that money and was such a nice person, I probably wouldn't mind lending him $1,000 so he could get false teeth. I burst out laughing when my friend read this. Who's an old man like him gonna bite?"

Some elderly abjured begging and sought advice about lotteries. Clinging to their pride, they were determined to avoid handouts. But putting faith in winning the lottery is misplaced indeed. Yet, they besieged winners with requests about where they normally purchased tickets, how many they bought, and what tips they could give which might help lower the odds.

Writers often asked winners to buy tickets for them. Several dollars might be enclosed along with self-addressed stamped envelopes, although some would-be winners simply asked people to send them tickets and promised to reimburse them. In some cases the volume of mail was so large that hundreds of dollars were received. Some requests were motivated by the belief that the handling of tickets by a winner might increase their chance of success, like the rubbing ritual. One winner was asked by two nuns he knew to touch their tickets.

"I thought they were kidding, but they were serious. I did it, but I said, 'The Lord doesn't answer my prayers for this anymore.' I didn't think it would work twice. They didn't win."

The story of a sixty-year-old retired widow who won a million dollars was told in a publication of the American Association of Retired Persons. She got so much mail she had to take an ad in the magazine thanking everyone for their good wishes and apologizing for not sending personal replies.

There were many offers to sell houses and real estate, as well as more esoteric items such as coin collections, jewelry, paintings, and antiques.

The variety of items and businesses people tried to hawk through the mail seemed limitless. Solicitations to buy insurance, stocks, grocery stores, pizza parlors, cars, and automobile franchises were received. Widows were common targets of marriage proposals.

"When I was on the David Susskind Show, we got to talking about this," said a sixty-year-old retiree. "I told him that I had twenty-five marriage proposals and he asked, 'By mail?' I said, 'By a few females, too!' "

Most people took such offhand overtures jovially, but some persistent suitors carried on a one-way writing campaign for months before accepting defeat. Some even followed up letters with phone calls. Such tactics annoyed and offended some of the elderly widows, especially those who had recently lost their husbands.

A seventeen-year-old high-school student was also pestered by aspiring suitors. One proposal came from a forty-year-old justice of the peace in Ohio, and was accompanied by a glossy photograph and biographical information. Matrimonial advances were not confined to females. A young bachelor millionaire was besieged after the newspapers carried a story on him. "I got letters and calls from all kinds of women. I'd like to think it was because of my looks, but I know better than that."

Proposals were directed not only toward the unattached;

married men were also propositioned. One forty-year-old father of four received a letter from an amorously inclined woman who suggested they could get together if he set the time and place. Another happily married father of three got a lengthy letter from a woman who was trying to interest him in her seventeen-year-old daughter, whose cuddly picture was enclosed. A million-dollar winner in New Jersey found himself in a compromising situation after his wife saw the following letter from his former girlfriend:

> Congratulations for your winnings.
> (but Bob, you were gonna marry me!!!!)
>
> Very Regretfully,
> Linda

"I tried to shrug it off, but it caused a little friction around here," he said ruefully.

Even peculiar requests, such as the following plea from an unhappy Filipino housewife in Canada, were not uncommon. (Accompanying her letter was a birthday card marked "Belated or advance," to cover all bases. "Since I come here, I'm wishing for an electric guitar for my oldest boy, secondhand only so he can play in band and stay off streets. My wish will come true if you spare me a little of your winnings.")

Letters came from around the world—Poland, England, Ireland, Brazil, Argentina, Greece, Israel, Italy, Czechoslovakia, Austria, West Germany, Spain, Puerto Rico, Mexico, Canada, and Australia. Language was no barrier to the writers, for if they couldn't speak English, they simply wrote in their native tongues. There were numerous letters in Polish, Italian, German, and French from Quebec.

A unique letter came to a seventeen-year-old high-school student from a young man in jail whose cellmates had bet him four cartons of cigarettes that she wouldn't answer. ("Besides I could really dig having a filthy-rich pen pal.") She wrote back and he won his bet.

Many writers identified with winners and offered reams of advice on what to buy, how to invest, where to travel, and what to see. These suggestions reflected the writers' own preferences, perhaps because they were trying to have the winners live out their own fantasies. They did not want the winners to fail, for their own wishes and aspirations were riding with them. They had to believe in someone and something—that there is a chance to change one's destiny; that there is hope for the future; that they might someday find themselves in a lucky situation.

Religiously oriented letters were often received, too. These carried blessings as well as biblical admonitions about lust and avarice. They were frequently laced with quotes from the Bible warning of the temptations Satan has in store. Pamphlets carrying spiritual messages were sometimes enclosed. A letter from a seventy-six-year-old widow from Iowa was sent to our seventeen-year-old high-school student, apparently because the writer perceived her as especially vulnerable. The writer quoted the Bible (Mark 8:36): "For what shall it profit a man, if he shall gain the whole world, and lose his own soul?" She concluded: "Search the new testament scriptures and Jesus will show you what to do."

While some people, like this woman, were sincerely trying to convey a spiritual message, others routinely acknowledged the Almighty in their requests for money. This may have been designed to assure winners of their righteousness before they popped the $5,000 or $10,000 question.

There were also many letters from confused, emotionally upset, or disturbed people. A New Jersey millionaire received a letter from a forty-year-old bachelor asking for "a grand so I can get married to my girlfriend. I have never been married, but I'm not a virgin. Please answer *soon* so I can make love under the *moon*."

Some correspondence was vicious and malicious, including blatant attempts to fleece winners, sometimes employing profanity, even threats. Such letters were seldom kept, but occasionally a humorous one was retained. One such letter requested $75,000 to produce the writer's show on Broadway and offered to list the winner as co-producer. "This could mean the start of a new life for you. There are loads of young actresses looking for work in New York, and they'll be beating down your door."

Many winners were already suspicious of writers' intentions. The letters did seem to follow a preconceived pattern, typically opening with a friendly greeting and a congratulatory statement to establish rapport. This was followed by a sorrowful story which linked sentimentality, loyalty, health, perseverance, physical and/or social deprivation with financial exigency. Because of the similarity of the letters, some winners were completely unreceptive to them. One millionaire never read them because he believed they were part of an organized plot:

"I heard about this group of con men. They write letters to all the winners to see what they can get out of them. They're all tied in together. That's why those letters winners get are pretty much the same. At the end of the year they get together and pool their take and split it."*

Most winners, however, read and were touched by the letters. Although not certain of their authenticity, they perceived that the thematic similarities might be attributable to the common problems confronting the poor and the aged. But while they sympathized with the pathos and deprivation portrayed in them, I know of no one who sent money. As one millionaire explained:

"How do you respond to them? Do you send the money? You can't be sure if they're on the level or trying to con you. Even if they needed the money, it's impossible to give to everybody who asks for it. Why, I got hundreds of letters. They came from all over the country, even from France and Italy. They came from all kinds of people, even priests. I got letters with pieces of palm in them. But it was always the same message: give me some money.

*Conversations with FBI agents in charge of fraud did not support this.

"I'd like to help people. They seem so sad and so much in need, but why does it have to fall on us? We never had any money either, and now this. There's only so much you can do. Their needs are so great. Why, we totaled up the requests one time. How much do you think they came to? $250,000! And they're still coming. Four years after we won, they're still coming. Just as it starts to die down, there's a newspaper story about some winner and it starts up all over again. We moved here to get some privacy and live in a beautiful place where we always dreamed we could live. Now that we're here, we have this. My uncle, he lives in this town and he has the same name as me, and he gets a lot of this mail. I feel bad enough when they come to me, but why does *he* have to be bothered? It makes me ashamed."

Those who believed the letters were authentic were anguished. To know of the suffering people were going through, to see them beg and degrade themselves, and yet not help, often filled them with remorse. It tempered the joy of winning into a mixed emotion, adding a little pain to their pleasure.

Though winners seldom replied, never gave money, and frequently did not bother to read the requests, the letters kept coming, even when the writers had the wrong address. Just like the celebrities they admired, winners found they received mail simply addressed to their name and general locale—e.g., "Buffalo—Suburban," or "Philadelphia area." These encroachments conflicted with their intense desire to preserve their privacy and greatly complicated my attempts to interview them. One man denied winning after I went through an elaborate explanation of the study. "I don't know what you're talking about. Nobody won any money here." Then he allowed me in, explaining, "I'll deny anything to strangers."

Many of the younger couples lived in a constant state of anxiety about the safety of their families. "You don't know what kind of kooks are out there" and "They might even try to kidnap my kids" were common remarks. Some people were undoubtedly apprehensive because they received threats, but no one I know of was physically harmed or paid money to would-be extortionists. But the fear was real, and reinforced by crank calls and letters and by stories in the media about kidnappings of wealthy persons. One third of the winners were living anxious, isolated lives because of such fears, whether or not they had actually been threatened.

In an effort to escape the threats and harassment, many people uprooted themselves. Thirty millionaire families moved after winning, and although this was partly to realize life-long ambitions, the pursuit of anonymity and privacy was a paramount consideration. Moving represented a chance to escape the hounding reporters, incessant calls, and the envious, inquisitive, and exploitive horde. Yet, even moving did not remove the fear and anxiety, or afford them all the privacy they sought. To maintain their anonymity, they did not divulge their secrets to neighbors. This sometimes complicated relationships because they had to guard their conversation against thoughtless slips. People are suspicious and curious about a young family with no visible means of support settling in their exclusive neighborhood. Inquisitive neighbors frequently questioned winners about their source of income and sometimes queried their children to learn more about them. Elaborate stories were concocted to account for affluent life-styles, and children were carefully indoctrinated to preserve tranquillity.

Try as they may to protect their privacy, winners are invariably revealed. This usually happens unceremoniously in a public place—often the supermarket. One woman described the harrowing experience:

"We didn't plan to make a show of it. We bought this new house and had been living here for a few months when I was shopping one day in a local supermarket. I was in the checkout line and I thought a woman in the line looked familiar, but the woman she resembled was much heavier. I said to myself that it couldn't be her, but, sure enough, she stared at me and said, 'Florence! How have you been?' She came from where we used to live, and I was hoping she wouldn't say anything about the money. Then she asked me how we liked living in this area now that we were well off. The ladies on each side of me in the line were all ears. I told her we liked the area very much, and then she asked what we were going to do with all the money we won in the lottery. That was it! One of the other ladies turned around and said, 'You won the lottery?' My friend broke in and said, 'She won a million dollars!' I couldn't deny it right there. Then the other lady asked me where I lived and when I told her she said, 'Oh, I know where that is. We live right down the block from you!' The very next day a neighbor's kid told one of my sons in school that he heard we won a million dollars in the lottery."

Another winner was forced to reveal his secret to a local bank to obtain a mortgage for his expensive new home. He was assured that the information would be held in strictest confidence. A few days later the mayor of his new town met him at the post office. "He smiled at me and said he knew all about my lucky strike, but that the secret would never get out. Ha!"

We have seen how many people learned, to their dismay, that winning can be a mixed blessing. For some it is like a reverse Midas touch—everything they do turns sour. Others are too fearful to spend it. Ensconced in their expensive new homes in strange surroundings, suspicious of the motives of friends, neighbors, relatives, and strangers, they are often lonely. They live in a state of siege, of self-imposed isolation, afraid to use their winnings lest they call attention to themselves. They have won the battle against poverty and deprivation, but are losing the war; they are financial successes but social and psychological casualties.

CHAPTER 4

Work in the Lives of Lottery Winners

"All day long I'd biddy biddy bum . . ."
—From Tevye's song "If I Were a
Rich Man" in *Fiddler on the Roof*

For nearly fifty years Mitchell Ryder taught the Hawaiian guitar to students in Philadelphia and all the while longed to go to the Islands. His life was a continual struggle to make ends meet. He tolerated teaching, but preferred the scholarly pursuit of musicology, which he had to forgo, and resigned himself to catering to a procession of uninterested pupils coerced into taking lessons by achievement-oriented parents. The endless hours of unharmonious chords grated on him, but he endured the cacophony for the sake of putting bread on the table. All the while he dreamed of going to Hawaii.

Then, on a hot summer day four years ago, Lady Luck played his song to the tune of a million dollars. It was like a Walter Mitty daydream. No more scrambling to survive and scurrying to be on time for lessons; and no more forced disingenuous compliments to the parents of would-be Beethovens. Mitch immediately closed his studio and embarked on his lifelong fantasy—he fled from the humdrum world of smog and cities and escaped on an extended vacation to an island paradise. The effects have been dramatic. He lost weight; his blood pressure dropped; and his outlook on life brightened.

"My wife and I go to Hawaii every winter now and spend three months in Oahu. We rent an apartment and have a ball! We go out to dinner and see a show almost every night, and I'm still active in my music. I know a lot of people in the Islands and they want me to play and teach there. I do a little, but not much. I don't want to be tied down. If I give lessons, I have to be there at a certain time. That's not for me. They wanted me to play when I arrived there this winter. I said, 'Not on your life! This is my vacation!'

"I even bought some land. Four acres on the big island of Hawaii. We don't stay there because it's not developed yet. There's even an active volcano nearby. We can see the black lava all around."

He bought the land a few years ago as an investment for his children and grandchildren for $50,000. Today it is valued at $70,000. In ten years, he estimates, it will be worth half a million.

Mitch and his wife live the other nine months in a house in an exclusive suburb of Philadelphia which they bought with the winnings. It sits on a hill and is beautifully landscaped. The interior is comfortably furnished. Upstairs is a large music room with an electric organ, an accordion, several bass viols, and half a dozen new and vintage Hawaiian guitars.

"This place cost me $50,000, but it's worth $75,000 now. I put a lot into it—a new roof, aluminum siding. I didn't pay cash for it, just twenty percent down, and I still have my old house in Philadelphia. One of my brothers lives in it. I was told not to pay cash for this place because I can use the mortgage payments on the house and land to deduct from my taxes. I also put some money in the bank in ninety-day savings certificates.

"I used to have high blood pressure and hypertension. I weighed 286 pounds and my doctor screamed at me. I've lost forty pounds now and I don't have hypertension anymore. I have no financial responsibilities or worries at all. In general, this way your blood pressure has to be better.

"Before we won, my wife and I never took a regular vacation. We might take an extra day off once in a while to make a long weekend, but that was it. I had to stay around my music studio and teach. You couldn't take off when you wanted. We got married in 1933, in the middle of the Depression, and it was rough ever since. Several times I thought about quitting and going into something else to support my family. If I had it to do over again, I would probably go into something else because to do what I did you should stay single. It's unfair to your family. No matter how great an artist you are, there's no guarantee that you'll ever be able to support your family. Now things are better, and I want to leave something for my children and grandchildren. My lawyer was a specialist in investments. He covered all the investment angles with me. I've got the money divided down to the last heir. My son-in-law is the president of a bank. He tells me, 'Dad, we don't need any money. Why don't you just spend it and live it up? Have a good time?' I'll be sixty-six in August. I got it made as long as we keep our health."

Mitch appears to have made the most of his money and freedom. Realizing he is finally in the catbird seat, he is enjoying life to the fullest. Many of us have wondered what we would do if we suddenly found ourselves in Mitch's place, freed from the necessity of working, even though there is little chance we will ever realize such a fantasy. Lottery winners like Mitch have been thrust into that situation. They provide us with an intriguing illustration of what actually happens when people suddenly become financially independent of their jobs.

In my conversations with over 100 big-money winners I learned of many dramatic changes in their work habits, especially among million-dollar winners. These people will be the focus of this chapter unless otherwise indicated.

Fifty-four people who were employed full-time were directly affected by the million-dollar windfall (husbands, wives, and children), and *all but fourteen quit their jobs.* This was particularly surprising since they had very stable working careers prior to winning. On the average, the men had been earning slightly more than $12,000 and the women around $8,000. Even though they professed a liking for their jobs (only two reported being dissatisfied) they wasted little time getting out. Twenty-six people quit immediately. Men were four times more likely to continue working than women, probably because they had higher-paying, more interesting jobs, but even most of them quit.

Winners' jobs were diverse, ranging from waitresses and assembly-line workers to salesmen and proprietors. Although more white-collar workers remained employed, a majority of people in every occupational category quit, even those with jobs generally thought to be interesting and creative. This may be one of the most significant and revealing findings, since social-science literature abounds with surveys depicting workers as satisfied with their jobs. The behavior of winners screams out to us that there *is* something radically wrong with the nature of work in our society. That people instantly dropped an activity they had engaged in most of their adult lives should be cause for consternation and concern. Here, in the experiences of the instant millionaires, we learn why people work in dehumanizing jobs, and we also discover that life without some form of purposeful activity can be as stultifying as a dead-end job.

The breadwinning burden which most of us must bear was removed from the backs of these lucky few, and some, like Johnnie De Carlo, used the opportunity to take life easy. Johnnie had a tailor shop in the back of his house, which was located in a small city in southern New Jersey. He worked seven days a week from five A.M. to ten P.M.

"Many's the time I was pressing at ten, eleven at night. It was a hell of way to live. I never had a vacation in thirty years. I always had so much work I had to do."

But the day after he won, he took his sign down and ended his long years of toil.

"Now that I don't work, we're out almost all the time

somewhere. Before, I was always in the house working like a rat. I'd be sitting in that chair and people would come in and say: 'Don't you ever get out?' I bought three new cars in the last few years and never had a chance to drive them. My son drove them. I always bought the same make and color. I didn't want people to know I could buy a new car, so I got them to look the same. I made good money, but it was for double hours. Anyway, I never had a chance to spend it. I worked pretty cheap. What I hear they get today and what I worked for were nothing like the same. If I got what they get today, I'd be a millionaire in three years."

How did you build up such a business?

"It all started by word of mouth. You do a good job and people tell other people. I was apprenticed to learn tailoring. I even had my finger tied down by my teacher so I couldn't cheat while I sewed. You never learn enough in this trade. I was still learning when I quit.

"There are other tailors in this town, but I had lots of my own customers. My business was personal. I knew everybody by their first name. They'd all come and talk. They'd stay for an hour or so, but I kept working. I couldn't stop.

"People were all sorry I quit. They still drive by and ask me to fix their clothes—'I can't get my pants fixed.' I tell them if I do it for one, I'd have to do it for all. You've got to have pride in your work. That's what it's all about. I liked my work. I quit, but I planned to quit anyway in a couple of years. I was sixty and I was as high as I could go. If I was forty years old, I'd probably have continued working. I might not have worked so many hours, but I wouldn't have quit.

"When I quit, I gave everybody free cleaning. All the clothes I had there in the shop I did without charge. I remember a colored guy came in. He had a bill for about $20, and when I told him it was free, he couldn't believe it. But I was always generous, and I worked for everyone. I don't care what color you are, black, brown, everyone.

"People said to me after I won: 'I guess you won't be talking with us anymore.' That's not so at all. We live in a supposedly ritzy section now, but we don't put on any airs. We go out to eat once a week. People say: 'I bet you go out all the time.' I tell them the best food is at home.''

Johnnie lives in a large two-story house in an expensive subdivision on the outskirts of the city where he lived and worked all his life. As soon as you see it, you are struck by the beautiful landscaping. This is his work.

"Even in our old house I used to find time to garden. I had such beautiful gardens there that people would stop and look at them. They even offered to buy some of my plants. I brought some of the bushes over here—transplanted them. I know a guy, he's a landscaper. He came here and told me that he would charge $35,000 to do what I have done here. The prices of these plants are fantastic. They're selling these pachysandras for eighteen cents apiece. I've got thousands of them. I must have two to three hundred azalea bushes around the house. And I've even begun shaping some of the bushes into animals like at Disneyworld, except they cheat by using wire."

There were bushes in the form of a turtle, a deer, a duck, and an elephant. Johnnie not only had a green thumb, he knew the scientific names of the plants and had acquired quite a bit of technical information on gardening. Inside, on his porch, huge plants climbed the walls and reached across the ceiling. In one corner stood a ten-foot avocado tree, in another an array of cacti, and in a third a large rubber plant. There was also a standing terrarium filled with exotic mosses and plants.

What else do you do with your time?

"I paint. See those pictures of ships on the walls? I did them. They're in water color and not by numbers. I just see something I like and paint it, like that landscape over there."

The richness and variety of color made his paintings attractive. There were several of a ship weathering a storm at sea, set in different color schemes.

"Besides painting I like to work around the house and at my daughter's. I do paneling and tile work and fix all kinds of things. I also have some of my machines from the shop in the cellar. I fix our clothes for the heck of it. I like to work with clothes."

We went into the basement to see his workshop and vintage machines. He proudly described their functions and how he was able to perform intricate stitching that is a vanishing art.

Now that you have time for vacations, what do you do?

"Oh, we travel a lot. We take bus trips. We're going to Williamsburg this weekend. We've been to Canada, New Orleans. We go to Florida every winter for a few weeks. We drive down. I'm scared of flying. Every time you get ready to fly, there's a big accident."

The money allowed Johnnie to quit tailoring and develop other talents. But even now he fiddles with his old machines ("I just couldn't sell them") to maintain the skills he devoted his life to perfecting. His need to remain active has blossomed in his gardening, handy work, and artistry. His love for people, previously expressed in kind words and amiability, is now demonstrated with charitable gifts. He is deeply religious, and his reverence for life and sensitivity find expression in his landscaping, painting, and generosity.

A lifetime of routine is hard to change in a few years, and so Johnnie still rises at five, but rather than heading for a room in the back of his house, he is free to walk in his garden, paint, or just relax. Being an active person, he cannot remain idle, and his fear of flying restricts his travel. Consequently, he finds small tasks to occupy his time and hands. Although the winnings brought security, he has not taken the opportunity to relax fully. But he is happy, and his ebullient spirit would be irrepressible even if he had not won.

Winners like Mitch and Johnnie were nearing the age of retirement and quit working because they felt they deserved a respite. They referred to themselves as "early retirees." These nineteen people (ten men and nine women) were older (average age fifty-nine) than the twenty-one "quitters," whose average age was forty-two. They also had been working longer in their last jobs than the "quitters," an average of nineteen years compared to twelve, and believed in the virtue of hard work, but felt they had done their share. Since less than half of them would have received a pension, they would have had to continue working beyond sixty-two, because Social Security hardly provides enough money to retire on.

Four people probably had their lives prolonged by winning. They were tied to their jobs solely for money, and had severe health problems. Jack Nowak's demanding job was largely responsible for his deteriorating health. Then, one year ago, he and his wife, Alice, won a special lottery drawing in New York which assures them of $200 a week for life. They receive $10,400 annually and pay $2,800 in taxes. $208,000 is guaranteed, but Alice, now thirty-five, can expect to collect upward of $400,000.

"I didn't believe in lotteries," said Alice, "but I do now. The girls at work kept talking about the lottery. So I bought three tickets. One of my friends kept saying, 'Don't bother to check your tickets 'cause I have the number.' At work the night before the drawing I told her she was wrong. I was going to win because my ticket had a queer number on it."

Has your life changed since you won?

"It was scary," said Alice. "You didn't know what all that money was going to do to you. But really our lives haven't changed." Then almost as an afterthought, "Well, Jack quit his job last month." It was no coincidence either, since the lottery income equaled his salary.

Jack explained: "I didn't like the company I was working for. I was on call seven days a week, twenty-four hours a day. I was never home, and when I *was* home, the phone was always ringing."

His trouble started five years ago, when he left his job as the chief inhalation therapist at a local hospital. He had worked there for sixteen years.

"That's where we met, Alice and I. She still works there as nursing supervisor in the night shift from eleven P.M. to seven A.M., but I left. I thought . . . I tried to make a future outside of there—to make more money."

Jack became vice president of a new inhalation-therapy company. He had the technical expertise necessary to make the company go, but this proved to be a hardship: when an emergency occurred, he was invariably summoned.

"He spent time in the hospital last summer," said Alice, "and while he was being wheeled downstairs for tests, they were calling him."

The constant barrage of emergency calls left them no time for recreation and relaxation.

"It was too much," said Jack. "A lot of times I'd have to take off at three or four in the morning and have to leave the kids at home alone. I didn't have a vacation in the five years I worked with the company."

"We'd get a tent pitched and have to take it down," said Alice. "We were always interrupted by calls. We'd go for a ride and the beeper would sound. I haven't been able to see my eighty-five-year-old grandfather in five years, and he only lives in Syracuse."

Jack confided that the demands of his job estranged him from his children. "But I'm gettin' re-established with them. Now I'm just relaxing. I'm going hunting on Sunday. It's the first time I've been able to do that in five years."

The Nowaks' jobs also limited their social life. Since Jack was in and out most of the day and Alice worked nights, they had little time for friends and neighbors. In addition to this, there was a more ominous effect from Jack's job: "My nerves were shot. Now I'm finally calming down."

"Since he quit a month ago," Alice observed, "he looks a hundred percent better than he did. He was irritable before. He'd be grumpy around the house."

It was obvious the winnings had freed him from an onerous job—one that might have brought him to an untimely end. The Nowaks recognized this and are thankful the pressure was removed.

"Right now I'm satisfied with being unemployed. I'm just

getting to the point where I'm relaxing. I've got a lot of work to do around the house that I haven't done for five years."

"The first thing they said at his company when he won was 'I guess Jack won't be here much longer.' They were right! We spent all summer canning in preparation for his quitting. The basement is full now," said Alice exuberantly.

Jack's new routine seems to be having a salutary effect on the household. The children were all smiles when they returned from school, and Alice beamed: "He even cooks while I'm out. He'll have me so spoiled, I won't want him to go back."

Jack talks about going back to work eventually. In fact, he likes the kind of work he was doing.

"If the working conditions had improved on my last job, I would have stayed with them. I liked working with patients. I did a lot of work with kids who had open-heart surgery. You'd get kids that were dead and have to revive them. So many parents fed their kids methadone to keep them quiet. They'd bring them in and I'd go to work on them. I didn't like seeing a child die.

"I've worked all my life and I'm only forty-six. Eventually, I'm going to get back to the point where I want to go back and bring some money in. I'll probably take a job as an inhalation therapist in a few months. I've got the experience that will help me get a job quickly."

Whether Jack will return to work is problematic. There is a possibility he will become habituated to his life of leisure. As Ed Munson, another winner, put it, "The longer you stay away from it, the less desire you have to go back." This observation may be even more prescient in Jack's case because he recognizes that his work adversely affected his health and family. In fact, he still had not unwound. During our conversation he continually coughed and chain-smoked. He was red-faced, haggard, and obese, looking much older than his age. His family wants to keep him home, and they can fruits and vegetables in an effort to contain their spending and stretch the winnings. If they are unsuccessful, Jack will heed the economic compunction to work which might be his ultimate undoing.

At fifty-seven, Lester Parnes' situation was similar to Jack's with the exception that he won considerably more money—a million dollars—and this permanently relieved him of the fatigue and anxiety associated with working. Lester worked for twenty years with a large electronics company, first in laborer jobs and then as inspector. He had no college education.

"I realized I would be pushing brooms and doing similar unpleasant things all my life unless I made an effort to improve myself. That's why I asked an engineer to teach me about radios."

This knowledge enabled him to obtain the job of quality-control inspector, and although he was asked many times if he would like to move into a technician's position, he refused because he suffers from essential hypertension. He has had this since he was thirty-five, but over the years it has become increasingly debilitating.

"My heart keeps pumping hard all the time. It's enlarged. I've always considered myself totally disabled. Working as just a layman makes hypertension worse. I just about had it. I applied for disability, but couldn't get it. No one will give it to you. Even though they know high blood pressure causes strokes and heart disease. You can't even get life insurance. The same insurance companies that won't give you disability won't insure you either."

Lester earned around $8,000 a year and, although overtime was available, he could not do it because of chronic fatigue. At the end of a day he could barely make it home. Two years ago business slumped and he was laid off.

"I was unemployed for ten months and my benefits were just about to run out. I had to make a decision about retirement. I could retire early and get a lower pension, or use my recall rights and get a job again with the company when things picked up. Then I won the million dollars. . . . It eased the pressure of making a living, but I hadn't made the decision. Then they had a little spurt there and they recalled me. This was like a kick in the pants. I hoped I'd finally laid everything to rest, that I wouldn't be forced to decide between continuing or quitting. My supervisor called up and asked if I would come in and help him out. He was a very nice guy and needed my experience on this particular job. He checked on all the benefits I'd get if I went back—like I'd get a bigger pension. I went back for him. He told me I'd only have to work for six weeks until this job was finished. I wound up working eleven. I thought it wouldn't kill me, but it nearly did.

"Look, you have to be honest with yourself. People work because they have to. What are you going to do? Where are you going to go? Why does anyone work? For the money. For me—and I'm serious—I think there is no job that can help essential hypertension. The conditions have to be A-1, and nobody's going to offer that. If I weren't a sick man, I'd probably be in the $15,000-to-$20,000 bracket."

About a year and a half ago Rosemary Parnes decided to go to work. She began as an assembler in an electronics plant, worked for a year, and left for a similar job elsewhere. She had been there about six months when her husband won. She recalled she decided to let her husband go alone to the drawing.

"I didn't think he would win more than the $500 all finalists get, so I went to work. I worked ten hours that day. When I got home, he was on the phone in the kitchen and I knew something had happened. I heard him talking and saying, 'I don't want to discuss it.' I guessed it was with reporters. When he turned around, his face was white. I asked him, 'How much did you win?' and he said, 'All of it!' The next day I called up my boss and said, 'I'm not coming in today.'"

So the Parneses quit their jobs and are happier and healthier.

"I miss the girls but not the work," said Rosemary. "I figure that I did a good job by raising a family and having them turn out well."

Lester expressed his feelings this way: "I feel I've left the harness once and for all. I had enough for twenty years. Since I won at fifty-seven, I have enough to live to seventy-seven and that's more than I ever expected to live. It's a real life-extender. Before I won, I was wiped out, done for. If they recalled me, I guess I would have dragged myself back."

Although he is unemployed, he thinks it is generally important for people to work. "If you don't use your body, you degenerate. I've seen people retire in good health and go into depression. Then again, I've seen some people that did all right after they retired. I guess it depends on the kind of work you are doing. If you were a doctor or a lawyer and had a job that interested you, you'd probably want to continue working. Our jobs weren't that interesting, not factory work."

Rosemary ridiculed former President Nixon's admonition to take pride in your job regardless of the kind of work. "Like Nixon was saying, 'As long as there are jobs, you should take them.' I'd like to see him go do some of them. I'd like to see him empty bedpans and take pride in it."

Lester interrupted: "Well, all kinds of work are necessary. They'll never make this world a utopia, and there's work that has to be done, and you gotta go in that coffin worn out."

When the Parneses were working, they found the most satisfying thing about their jobs was the pay. Lester summed it up thus: "You can't wait till Wednesday,' cause then you only have two days to go to payday. The most dissatisfying thing was the regimentation. The whistle blows to eat and you're not hungry, but you have to eat anyway."

He recalled the day he won; the drawing was held at a racetrack.

"I've never been to a racetrack before. They wanted me to place some bets and I wouldn't do it. I don't approve of that form of gambling. They were asking me just for numbers after a while. They thought it was my lucky day. They asked, 'How could you say no when you buy lottery tickets?' I'll tell you why—I think buying lottery tickets is fair. There's no favoritism or loopholes. I was completely satisfied with the Jersey system. If you've got any gambling blood in you and a few spare cents, it's worth it."

A few years ago he tried another form of gambling. He invested in the stock market. "I took a bloodbath. I lost about $10,000. This experience had a lasting effect.

"I realize that in a few years, after the income-averaging is over, I'll be in the fifty-percent tax bracket. But I don't want to take any risks in investments. Even municipal bonds. All of these investments have some risk, and when there's risk, I don't sleep. And if I don't sleep, I'll die."

In their search for privacy the Parneses moved to a charming ranch house in an upper-class residential area near Philadelphia.

"Even here it's not free from vandals and thieves who prey on innocent people. You have to be careful. There are nice people out there, but there are also people who want to do you harm. Sometimes you take a chance, like with you, based on a judgment of your face. You looked honest. Some people would like to get in here—they think you have a lot of money in your home just lying around. They'd like to come in and take it. Why, they even called people around here on the phone and said they were from a burglar-alarm company and would they be interested in having an alarm system installed. They called one of my neighbors about this, and he told them he wasn't interested. He said he didn't need one. He said he had one of the best systems already installed, with the most modern equipment. In fact, he said he had three systems. Why, you couldn't even walk in his garden without touching off an alarm and alerting him to pick up his gun." (Lester has an alarm system in his house.)

So Lester and Rosemary are taking life easier now. "I don't do too much. Not that I don't want to," said Lester, "but I fear that I might get ill. Even if I went for a ride, I'm afraid that I might be too tired and I wouldn't be able to get home. Then there's always the possibility that I might have some kind of attack while I was driving. I suffer from chronic fatigue. I wish I could do more, but I can't. All I do is relax all day. For me I call it life. I do think it will extend mine."

"It was a blessing," said Rosemary.

Lester viewed work in purely economic terms. He wanted to improve his life, but his anxiety level conflicted with his ambition. Luckily, he won a lottery and was able to get out of the labor force, or else he would have had to endure the physical and psychological torture of his job until he succumbed. Lester's health problem may be exacerbated by his hypersensitivity to others' motives vis-à-vis his money. To protect himself from the onslaught of the public and his hypertensive condition, he remains at home, in self-imposed isolation, with his burglar alarm connected.

Two other winners, Minnie Petraglia and Wilma Kovaleski, whom we will meet in our discussion of widows (Chapter 5), also had debilitating health problems and were released from the rigors of work by their wins. Had they been forced to continue working, they, too, would probably have suffered severe physical and emotional trauma. It is not exaggerating to say the money seems literally to have saved these people's lives.

Some winners left their jobs because of other kinds of pressure. For example, there were numerous reports of dramatic changes in co-workers' and supervisors' attitudes toward them. Many perceived a chilled atmosphere in their workplace, like the one Seymour Landen encountered. Seymour is thirty years old and won a million dollars three years ago. He lives in a sparsely populated area on a dead-end street. His house, a nine-year-old split-level, is the last one on the block and sits on the edge of a forest. I rang the bell and he answered.

"I don't believe it! They said wherever I moved you'd find me, but I didn't think it was possible." He was visibly disturbed, and his wife stood anxiously by, importuning him not to speak with me.

"I don't want anybody to know I won. People out there are funny when it comes to money. You and me didn't live through the Depression, but I've talked to people who did. If you've got to survive, you'd do anything to help yourself and your family. You don't know what people would do if they found out. They might even try to kidnap my kids.

"We're here just two years and nobody knows. We used to live in [a major industrial city], but when I won we decided to move. We got in the car and kept riding. There was a ring around the sun, and I told my wife we would drive until we couldn't see it anymore. We stopped when it disappeared, and this is the place. It's sort of out in nowhere—a real change from where we used to live. The TV stations! They go off and on all the time, and the local paper comes out only once a week. I view this as a temporary move, just like my being unemployed is temporary.

"I don't have many friends here. It's tough to get to know the people. They have lived here a lot longer. A lot of them are farmers and they stick together. I joined the Volunteer Fire Company recently. I'm not working and I figured I had the time to help out. Come with me to the station. I have to do something I promised them."

We drove there in his Chevrolet Nova. As we pulled into the lot, he cautioned, "If anyone comes in, don't say anything about the lottery. Nobody knows around here. Not even my neighbors, and that's the way I want to keep it." The station was deserted. There were two new engines and one ancient pumper. Seymour is a talented mechanic and had promised to repair a broken high-pressure hose on the pumper. As he worked, we talked about his life and plans.

"I'm a high-school graduate and I took some night courses in college, but I didn't like it. I remember one night, when I was sitting in class, I heard this loud screech and a bang. I had a feeling that my car had just been hit. I left the class and, sure enough, some drunk had plowed into it. It was demolished. I never went back.

"I didn't care for college, so I started looking for work. I learned how to be a draftsman. I picked it up by taking many different jobs. I'd never stay at one, just long enough to learn something new, then I'd move on. On my last job I was being trained in the design of pressure vessels and pipe support systems. It's in the area of heat-exchange systems for cooling plants and power generating. I was commuting two hours each way every day, but the money was good. I was deep in debt and on this job I could earn $300 to $500 a week."

You quit your job even though you liked it and were making good money?

"In one week the attitude of the guys at work changed. They got quiet. I sensed something. It wasn't all the guys, but there was something there. I took a week off from work, and when I returned, I felt something wasn't right. I went home that Monday night and thought it over. I might have stayed if it had been different. I wasn't forced out. I made my own decision. The boss didn't want me to leave. He liked my work, but he said he understood.

"Some of the trouble at work was around how I got the winning ticket. I had never bought any tickets before because it was taking bread off the table. To me, it was a waste. I could get two loaves of bread or two quarts of milk for a dollar. One of the guys at work sold lottery tickets and he wanted to know if I wanted any. I just bought two—the only tickets I ever bought that I can remember. One of them was the winner. When I went back to work, a lot of guys wanted to know what the odds were against me winning. I told them that it was only fifty-fifty, because either God is going to give it to you or He's not. I figured without God's help I wouldn't have half the things I have. I'm a Catholic. I prayed for good fortune, but I just said, 'If it's possible, I'd like to win.'

"When I returned to work, there was a lot of scuttlebutt at the office about how I should give the guy who sold me the ticket some money. First they were saying I should give him a few hundred. Then it became a few thousand. Then it was $5,000, then $10,000, and then $15,000. I just cashed my paycheck and went up to the guy. He had a real good job there. He was clearing at least $500 a week, sometimes as much as $750. I went to him and gave him a $100 bill. He held it in his hands, looked at it, then handed it back and said, 'You take this, Seymour, and think it over.' I think the guys at work had needled him until he expected a lot more.

"After he gave me the money back, I left. I thought about why he gave it back. Then I decided to give him more. But I couldn't get the $50,000 check cashed. I went to one bank and said, 'Here's my check and here's my picture in the paper. I want a couple hundred dollars and I'd like to put the rest in your bank.' They wouldn't cash it for me. I wanted to know why, and the man explained to me that if the check got lost in transit they'd be in lots of trouble. I went to three banks and nobody would cash it for me. Not even my own bank. They gave me the same kind of story.

"A couple of months later, after we moved, I sent the guy some money. I had just sent a check in the mail when the next day I got a card from him. I don't know how he got my address. It was a strange card. I opened it up and all you could see was a black background and a white picket fence that ran across it. There were two eyes staring through the fence, and underneath it he had written, 'I'm in the dark about the $.' I yelled out, 'Why, that son-of-a-bitch!' He had a lot of nerve. I even thought about stopping payment on my check, but I let it go. You know, I never even got a thank-you.

"I thought a lot about why things cooled toward me at work. Maybe I should have said, 'Come on, let's all go out to lunch.' I've often wondered whether their attitude toward me was that way because I didn't take them out to lunch. Or was it because I didn't give the guy as much money as he thought I should? Or was it because they felt I was taking money away from someone? I've been thinking about it. These are the only reasons I've come up with."

Do you buy tickets now?

"No. I might if the local paper carried the winning numbers, but they stopped doing that. A funny thing happened here recently. I was sitting here and the lounge was pretty well filled with people. A guy came over to me and pointed to a fella near the end of the bar. He said to me, 'See that fella there? He won $50,000 in the lottery.' I said, 'No kidding. I wonder what he did with all his money.' I could hardly keep from laughing."

You haven't worked, then, since you quit your job two years ago?

"That's not exactly right. I do odd jobs when I want to. Some last for a few days, some for a couple of weeks. If I find something I'm interested in, I do it. You're not going to learn everything from talking to somebody.

"I've looked into many things. I've been thinking about investing in some business, but there always seems to be something wrong with them. I've checked into McDonald's, Dairy Queen, a grocery chain. I'm thinking about something now. It will mean that I'll be my own boss, and I want a job that will allow me to be with my family. It depends on how much time I want to put into it. I could make from $15,000 to $75,000. Then I could work hard and it might only come out to making seventy-five cents an hour, but I don't mind. A job is not a way of life, it's a means of attaining it. I believe work is healthy for you. It's the best thing for you. Look at these farmers around here. They're seventy and eighty years old—healthy. There's a man eighty-six. He lives down the road. He walks back and forth to his son's place every day. He's healthy because he's active.

"When I find the right thing, I'll know it and I'll do it. When you have something available to you that you didn't have before, you like to explore the possibilities. Right now I'm living for today. This is life and I'm enjoying it. I like to think I live each day as it comes, and I try to practice this. I don't even have enough time now to do all the things I want. I need a couple of twenty-six-hour days. Of course, it's quite possible that a person in my position could end up looking for twenty years."

Although he is not overly ambitious, Seymour would like to remain active. He is young and skilled, but wants to make the right decision before investing his time, money, and energy. His reticence is bolstered by his suspicion of others' motives and his disinclination to work for someone. Perhaps more significantly, his comments reflect a pecuniary interest in work: "A job is not a way of life, it's a means of attaining it." Freed from bosses, a four-hour commute, and the financial crises characteristic of young couples' lives, he is savoring his independence. But he is lonely and isolated—a big-city boy in a tightly knit rural community. If he remains and wants to keep his secret, he will have to start working, or people will ask questions about his source of income and spurn him as a loafer. If he returns to the city, where he can retain his anonymity, he might never return to work—a thought which obviously has occurred to him. Realizing he does not need the income derived from a job, he acknowledges he may continue drifting aimlessly.

Seymour left his job even though he did not have serious problems with co-workers. Whether the hostile atmosphere he sensed was real or would have led to more serious difficulties is irrelevant, because he, like other winners, anticipated problems and acted accordingly. But there were many concrete examples of contentious co-workers and frustrating experiences on the job. A large proportion of these were reported by women.

Two waitresses had similar difficulties. After being pressured by co-workers, one quit and the other reduced her hours from forty to eight a week. Both contended they had wanted to continue working full-time and were bored with their enforced idleness. As one lamented, "The other waitresses resent me. They feel I'm taking money away from somebody else. They make you feel guilty. It's only the working people that resent the fact I'm still there, and I love that kind of work. There are some very well-to-do people that come to the club I work at. They know that we won and they treat me very nice. Eventually, I'll have to stop."

The experience of Lorraine Matisse, who was working part-time as a legal secretary when she and her husband won $200,000, is likewise revealing. "The day after I won, the supervising secretary had a girl in the office, interviewing her for my job. We had never gotten along very well, but I was shocked. She was trying to use my winning as an excuse to dump me. I told the boss about it. He said loudly, so she could hear, 'You're staying until you want to leave.' I stayed on a year longer, and then I left on my own terms."

Women may have had more interpersonal problems than men because of the intense competition among low-skilled females for jobs and the jealousy from women co-workers who envied their freedom. Feminist rhetoric notwithstanding, many middle-aged women are content to remain home, and the winners were not exceptions. They had worked primarily to supplement their husbands' income, and many preferred the comfort and security of their homes and the housewife role to the dullness and hostility of their jobs.

Men, however, were not immune from the gossip and ridicule of co-workers, as Carl Braun learned. A foreman glassblower in a large plant in northern New Jersey, he was shocked at the immediate repercussions from his win.

"When I came back the day after we won, one fellow who had worked for me for twenty-five years passed out on the job. He fainted dead away right there. I had to take him to the hospital. I think he was afraid that I might quit and he wouldn't know who his boss would be. Actually, he had nothing to fear. I've done this work for thirty-five years and I wouldn't dream of giving up my job. Of course, in the beginning you think what fun it would be to quit, but your work is really important to you. A lot of people don't feel that way, though. They resent that you continue working. Yes, they resent it. They want you to do what they would do. But I'm only fifty-two and I couldn't see dropping out of the picture. Work is something you actually need to do. That's why you hear of people being bored to death when they retire, and people dropping dead. Work makes you get up in the morning. Life would be too boring without it, and I make out good there [$22,000 a year]. But if I had it to do all over again, I guess I'd like to do something less hazardous."

Obviously, Carl worked for more than money, and he was

not going to let co-workers force him out. While complaints about co-workers were common, a few winners reported a change in the attitude and behavior of management, too. For example, a soap salesman of twenty-eight years continued working for a year and a half after winning, and did not get another raise, although previously he had received one every nine or ten months. Such unexpected ramifications sometimes go beyond the immediate beneficiary of the win. When Minnie Petraglia won a million dollars, her thirty-four-year-old son suffered a setback.

"My mother did all right in her job, but *I* never got another raise. I was working as an accounting clerk and I got $30 a week in raises in my first six months, and then she won. The next two years I got none. I don't work there anymore. I probably would have left anyway, but not getting any raises helped make up my mind."

Sometimes winning had a salutary effect on working. A few people reported that their effectiveness on the job actually increased. Tom Galen, a fifty-seven-year-old maintenance foreman, found he was able to use his new independence to his advantage; he could handle people more easily and command their respect.

The Galens won a million dollars a year ago in the Pennsylvania State Lottery. Although Tom is only five feet four, he possesses considerable energy which he channels into his work. He proudly explained the many facets of his job.

"I'm a maintenance foreman at my plant. I supervise about ninety people in the foundry—crane repairmen, machine repairmen. I'm also responsible for hiring some of these people. I've worked there for thirty-three years. I'm in charge of several divisions of maintenance, and it's very difficult for one man to handle them all. But I've learned by working in all of them. I climb up on cranes and do everything, all kinds of stuff. Many times I ask myself how the hell I do it—cranes up above, people below. I could walk out of there tomorrow. The place gave me a living when I needed it, and I'm not running away from it. I wouldn't ask my people to do anything I wouldn't do, and they respect me for this.

"There's enough responsibility there right now. If I leave there tomorrow, they'll put three men on to handle my job. They'll even tell you at the shop, 'You want to get something done, see Tommy.' People ask me how I handle all of them. Guys tell me they'd just take one of the jobs, wouldn't spread themselves thin. But I love the work I'm doing. When I won the money, they [management] said to me, 'I suppose you're going to leave us.' They didn't think I would stay.

"I work six days, sixty to seventy hours a week. I leave home at six fifty in the morning and come back at five. Sometimes, like last week, I get called in on emergencies and don't get home until ten or eleven.

"I spend most of my free time working around the house, and I'm part owner of another house which I help to fix. Sometimes on the way to work or after it I'll stop at my aunt's house and cut the lawn. I'm planning to put in a new porch there and paint her house this summer. I guess I don't have that much time to sit around. My family gave me a set of golf clubs, but I haven't used them yet.

"I used to worry, you know, if the work wouldn't get done, but not now. It doesn't affect my nerves now because I don't let it. They [management] listen to me more now, since I won. Before, they looked at me as just a worker when I made a suggestion. Now they feel, 'There's money behind him. He doesn't have any special reason other than pointing out the way for us.' People above used to look down on you. Now they're glad to talk to you. You can sense this when you're with them. They listen and figure, 'He must be doing it for the benefit of the company.'

"It's easier handling people, too. Before, you'd tell them [lower-level workers] ten times and get action maybe four. Now you get it eight or nine out of ten. If a guy doesn't want to do the work, I tell him, 'It's all right because it's your job that'll be lost if they close up, not mine.' I get more work out of the worker and it's good for the company, too. Many times I walk up to people and say, 'Hey, you don't give a damn, neither do I.' Younger people in particular don't care. They don't take the interest that the older people did. They run to the unions more.

"Two or three guys at the shop said, 'Why did *you* win— we could have used it more than you.' I was surprised at this —they were office people, not workingmen. They were educated and I didn't expect it of them."

What kind of changes have occurred in your life since you won?

"My biggest change, I bought this car—a Continental. I take it to work and the guys really rib me. Some of the younger guys will say maybe ten times a day, 'Dad, what do you say—adopt me.' The manager in my section kids me, 'We need a million here for this project. Well, the only guy who understands what this is about is Galen—he's got it. I'm the only manager in the area with a millionaire working under him.' "

One is struck by Tom's commitment to his job, his pride in doing it well. Not only does he put out 100 percent, he expects others to do so. He obviously derives a sense of accomplishment from working, and one might conclude that life without it would be unthinkable, but his final remarks are revealing:

"I'm fifty-six now and looking forward to getting out in a year. It [the money] is beginning to give me a broader view. I'm getting up there in age. Look, you got a few dollars and if you don't spend now, you won't be able to later."

Even "workaholics" need a rest, and after a lifetime of double-duty performance on the job, Tom is thinking about quitting, but he is not the kind of person who will be content with idleness. The placid life that awaits him may well force him back into the turmoil of the workplace.

A few of the younger winners, like José Vadilla, initially quit working only to return. José was thirty-seven when he won four years ago. After being out of work for nearly two years, he realized he was too young to remain idle and now works harder than ever.

José was raised on a farm in rural Puerto Rico, where life was not easy. Long hours of hard work yielded only a subsistence income. Like many of his countrymen, he came to the mainland to seek a better life. Although he had not finished high school, he could speak English. When he arrived, he wandered around for a while and then joined the Marines. After his tour of duty he spent seven years in the merchant marine. He did not earn much, but the experience was invaluable because he learned plumbing, carpentry, and electrical skills. When he left, he settled in Philadelphia, and with the money he had managed to save he opened a small hardware store in the Puerto Rican community. It was not a large-scale operation, making only $5,000 to $6,000 a year, but he enjoyed it. The hours were long because he would often assist customers making repairs. His wife worked full-time as a secretary-bookkeeper, and together they managed to survive the frustration and depression around them and raise three children.

Some of José's winnings were used to purchase a tavern, where he puts in long hours. It is located on a main street on the fringe of the Puerto Rican community in Philadelphia. The building is old and dimly lit, but the forty-foot bar with its highly polished wooden surface shone through the smoke and darkness. The ceiling was hung with white acoustical tiles, and the walls were freshly painted. I found José huddled in a corner watching two patrons shoot pool.

"I bought this place six months ago. It was a real dump. It took me six months to fix it up. There was a stairway in the middle of the room and I took that out and put in the ceiling. It made the room look twice as big. I put in all new plumbing and rewired the place. Now I'm fixing upstairs. I'm going to make it into a night club. It's the nicest bar around here. Right now I have mostly white customers, but it's mixed. The Puerto Ricans are moving up and in a couple of years it'll be all Puerto Rican."

Your wife told me you quit working after you won.

"I sold the first hardware store. The hours were long, eight in the morning to eight at night. When I quit, I was thinking it was easy life for me, but it wasn't. Before, I was working hard. I hoped I would improve. Then, when I won, I thought I had a lot of money and quit. That was a big mistake. I got very bored. I was out of work for twenty months and then bought another hardware store. I still have it, but I'm trying to sell it now. My wife works there. She works hard. She used to work as a secretary in a hospital before I won. Now she helps me out with the paperwork here. I leave all the books to her. She takes care of that. She is my right hand.

"Now I work fifty to sixty hours a week, sometimes more. Sometimes I take home only $50. I don't tend bar. I got a bartender and a barmaid. I'm the manager.

"I work to keep occupied, and I'm trying to build something big for the future—for my kids. When I won, the reporters asked me, 'How come you are so cool?' I told them this is nothing for me. I worked hard all my life. This is a future for my kids. I'd like them to get a good trade and a good education—to be doctors and lawyers. I was poor when I came to this country. I want them to have more. One of my sons, he's very smart. He got one of the highest test scores in the city. We hope to send him to a school for special kids. You have to have certain scores to get in. My older son is sixteen. He's six foot tall. And my daughter—she's three. I spend a lot of time with my little girl. She's my life."

José is well on the way to providing a secure future for his children. He has purchased fourteen houses in the city's core areas at bargain prices and repairs them at minimal cost. A few months ago he bought a dilapidated restaurant in an industrial section. "I hope to get it fixed up and open it in six months. There's a factory right by it. Eight hundred people work there and they're going to come to my place for lunch."

Having risen from poverty, he is keenly aware of the problems facing his friends in the Puerto Rican community. He subsidizes various community services and donated a home to a long-dormant Puerto Rican social club. "They hadn't been doing anything for a long time. I was hoping to get it

started again. It's for all people in the Puerto Rican community, older people and children. They can play baseball and
do everything there."

His civic-mindedness has not gone unnoticed. He is well
liked and has been approached to run for public office. "They
came and asked me if I would run for State Representative.
I told them I'm not qualified. They said it didn't matter, that
everybody would vote for me. But I can't speak well. I would
like to learn to speak better, and I would like to learn more
about bookkeeping to see where my money goes."

José has a combination of background characteristics that
normally would condemn someone to the nether world of
the labor force in our society. Though poor, lacking education, and a member of a minority group, he was able to
transcend these handicaps; and, through perseverance,
shrewd investments, and luck, he may ultimately become
rich.

Marty Timmons, a gas-station manager, also kept working
even though his job is not very lucrative, because: "Work is
something I'm used to, and I just can't get away from it. A
job gives you independence. You don't have to rely on anybody else for food and clothing. When you get married, you
need a job to support your wife and kids."

Marty is forty-one, and in the two years since he won he
has not missed a day of work. He puts in sixty to seventy
hours a week, pumping gas and doing minor repairs.

"I used to be open on Sundays, but the gas shortage killed
that. When it was over, I couldn't find anybody to work on
Sundays. I had a lot of trouble during that shortage. A couple
of guys threatened to beat me up. Some said they would
come back later and wreck the station. That's the most dissatisfying thing about this job—when customers come in and
complain. They want to be waited on first and they're last in
line. They drive you right up the wall. You'd like to tell them
off, but you can't."

How does working here affect your nerves?

"It depends. Some days . . ."

His wife, Martha, was listening and interjected: "Sometimes he gets headaches from the tension."

Marty continued: "Business is slow now. I don't need the money, but you want the station to pay its own way. I haven't been getting many headaches lately."

When was the last time you got one?

"Yesterday," he said, smiling. "It seems I get them when I sleep too late. I don't know why."

Business was indeed slow. Only four cars came in during the three hours we spoke.

How much did you make before taxes last year?

"About $12,000. I average $8,000 to $12,000 a year. I was too young to retire. I'd like to retire when I'm fifty-five. But I like my job. I think it's the greatest. It gives us stuff I wouldn't have if I still worked in the steel mill. I did that for five years. They were always laying me off. I always wanted a service station for as long as I can remember. You're always learning here. Cars come out different every year. Different motors, different electronics systems. You always got something to learn here. By rights, I should be going back to school. With these new systems coming out, it's hard. They're going in more for electronics."

You've received two checks so far. What did you do with the money?

"I got a couple of hospital beds for my two nephews. One of them is sixteen and one is eighteen. They have muscular dystrophy and needed these special beds. They're electric. I give other relatives things they need, too. I bought that new Ford Crew Cab for $6,500, but the main thing was the house. We used to live in Levittown, but when we won we bought a new house. The whole first check went for that. It cost $120,000. I've invested about $20,000 in municipal bonds and we bought new furniture for around $10,000. My wife wants to carpet the third floor now."

Their "new" home is a three-story colonial faced with stone, situated on four acres of land. About twenty-five yards in front and to the left are the remains of a stone barn.

Farther to the left is a huge tree recently cut, with a few logs nearby. In the rear is an empty pool. The house did not look overly expensive.

Martha took me on a tour of it. "You know, after we found we were in the finals, the first thing Marty did was give the two $500 checks he got to his nephews so they could get those electric beds. He didn't think he was going to win anything else, but figured he never even expected to get this, so he gave it to them."

As we walked, she displayed the spacious rooms and a majestic spiral stairway which curled upward through the center of the house. The floors were hand-made with boards of varying widths.

"The new section of the house was built in 1834. That's what it says on the cornerstone. The old part was built in the 1700's. We've got a lot of work to do here yet. Marty's refinishing that stairway over there. It seems to never end. When someone asks you what your mortgage payments are, they don't believe you."

How much are they?

"$975 a month."

Where did you get the money for the down payment?

"We sold our old house for $26,000 and used that plus a lot of the first check. Looking back on it now, we should have stayed in Levittown a couple more years and paid that house off. We had a nice yard there, too. Then we could have taken our time and found the right place. We have a lot to do here."

Although Marty is committed to his job, one senses that their financial needs figure prominently in his devotion. Taxes on his winnings have been averaging $20,000 a year. This leaves them with $30,000, from which they pay approximately $12,000 for their mortgage. Other expenses account for several thousand more, leaving them with about $15,000. It is obviously in Marty's interest to make the station successful.

Although he is an easy-going, good-natured fellow, the pressures and anxieties about his station have been getting to him. He complains of headaches and is obviously worried about the future. In the office, over shelves containing cans of oil and assorted engine additives, hangs his framed millionaire certificate for all to see. Perhaps it is there to reassure him about the eighteen future installments. In the meantime, he struggles to meet his exorbitant expenses and continues serving time at the pumps.

Much interest has focused on the alienation of people from their jobs in industrial societies. Ed Munson, sixty-three, a wizened but colorful ex-setup man, personifies this condition. Ed worked for the last sixteen years in a factory near his home, and had responsibility for preparing and running machines. He lives in a decrepit two-family house on the fringe of the black ghetto in a heavy-industry city. His Oldsmobile 98 stands out incongruously among the assorted clunkers of his neighbors. On the small plot in front of his house is a "FOR SALE" sign. It was one P.M. when I climbed the front steps and rang the bell. Ed opened the door a few inches and peered out, squinting at me with bloodshot eyes. The house was in darkness. On the living-room floor was a pile of clothes.

"Come in and sit down on that sofa there. We're moving out of this place, but I'll talk to you."

Are you still working?

"Hell, no! I quit three years ago. I wanted to quit right away, but my foreman persuaded me to stay awhile. There were only four of us who knew how to run and set up the machines. He asked me to stay on and break in a new man. He said it would be for only a couple of months, but then he started talking me into staying on longer. He said I was near my vacation time and I deserved to get it because I already put in a lot of time. Guys would say to me, 'What the hell are you doing here?' The owner of the plant would nod his head and shake my hand. I'd just smile. I knew I could walk out of there anytime. I wound up staying there for eight months. If I let that guy keep talking, I might still be there."

They gave you vacations?

"Not really. They gave you $200 or $300 and asked you to keep working. Then they'd take off a week every year to clean and fix the machines and furlough you. It just didn't pay for me to stay there after I won. I was only making around $5,000 a year. I'd be working for my Uncle [Sam]. He'd take most of what I'd earn, so it didn't pay to work.

"Let me tell you, I don't miss being away from it either. The longer you stay away from it, the less desire you have to go back. I'm not afraid of work; even though I never got past the eighth grade, I've had more than a college education— a practical education *out there*. I went to the school of hard knocks. I have nine kids, and you had to work hard and do everything yourself to survive. I spent most of my life working as a laborer in all kinds of different jobs. For three years near the end of World War II, I drove tractor-trailers during the day and worked in a factory at night. I worked seven days a week, eighteen hours a day. I averaged two hundred miles a day in the trucks. It's not easy driving those trucks. You can't stop them in an emergency when you have a load on. And you're always afraid of losing your license. I stopped it, though. Business fell off, so I gave up.

"Jobs are nothing but worries. You have to get up in the morning to get to your job, and you worry about being sick and whether the kids are sick and, if you have to miss work, whether they'll dock your pay or fire you. You worry about getting to work on time, and you don't know if the old car will start. Let me tell you, there's always pressure in a job. And you always got some rats there spying on you. There's always someone looking over your shoulder. When you go into these factories, no one teaches you. If you want to learn, you have to watch. So I'd just keep my eyes open.

"You know, every job varies. Most aren't any good. Mine was just one step above a laborer. I was only waiting to get out of there. You don't advance with these brown-nosers around there. Why, nine out of ten people are limited in what they can do, so in order to get ahead, you've got to have

the drive and work for yourself. But no one ever got any-
where working for somebody else. The only thing to do is be
in business for yourself. That's the only way to get ahead.

"Jobs are something you have to do to be able to survive.
The most dissatisfying thing about my job was having to be
there. I was never satisfied with any job I ever had. Even
when I was painting, I used to lay in bed at night thinking
where I was going to start in the morning and how I could
finish on time. That's all you do in your job, scheme and think
of ways to get out of there and get it over with. And even
when you come up with good ideas, they don't give you
credit for it. I once showed my foreman how to set up a
machine by using a hoist. You could lift the thing and slide
it into position just right. He said it wasn't any good, but a
month later he had us doing it in front of the boss to show
him *his* new idea. That's why I keep my own ideas on the
outside of the plant and not the inside. But I always had
self-respect. If you haven't got that, you go easy.

"The guys I was working with didn't make things any
easier. They were losers. They had a thousand-man turnover
there a year. It was a very dangerous job. I seen guys lose
hands and fingers. One guy lost all his fingers when the press
came down on his hand.

"One day I was talking with this new guy, showing him
how to run the machine. The boss came over and started
yelling at me because he was smoking. 'Munson, didn't you
tell him not to smoke here?' I told him I was too busy and
forgot. (The boss hated smoke. He had this thing about it. He
had lung cancer and died from it later.) He looked at this guy
and said, 'Don't you know smoking is bad for you?' The guy
looked at him and said, 'So what? So I die from lung cancer
and you die of ulcers from worrying about all your money.'
He wasn't there the next day.

"Why, they had more morons at that place than I ever seen
in my life. I think he got them out of the bughouse. I remember one time I was showing a guy how to lift a piece of
equipment with a block and tackle. I set it all up and pulled

the chain to raise it as he watched. Then I climbed up to push it where I wanted it and yelled down to him to lower it. He looked at me and asked how. Why, if I raised it by pulling one of the chains, how the hell are you going to lower it unless you pull the other one!

"Another day a colored guy who worked there came in late. He was really drunk. He wandered around for a while and then went upstairs somewhere and fell asleep. When he woke up, it was in the middle of the night. There were no lights on and the place was empty. 'Where is I? Where is I?' He got down to the front door and started opening it and tripped the burglar alarm. Police came from all over and arrested him.

"I guess you can't expect to get much better help. They only pay them around $2 an hour. I started there at $1.50 in 1957, and when I left two years ago I was making $3 an hour and I was even in a union. Why, it's the unions that are ruining this country. They keep jacking up wages and then this gets passed off to everyone in higher prices.

"But I'd like to forget about all that now. Right now I'm enjoying my retirement. I'm almost one hundred percent satisfied. The only trouble is if I don't move around, it becomes monotonous—you know, if you sit around all the time. You got to have something to do. That's why I travel a lot. I just got back from Florida. I drove to California and back twice. I been to Mexico, Nassau, Canada, Maine. . . ."

Ed's comments are filled with contradictions. He was dissatisfied with his job because it did not pay enough, but it was also uninteresting and did not afford him the freedom to be creative. This alienated him from his job and, perhaps, from people in general. However, he still believed in the virtue of work and proudly recalled his stable working career, his industriousness and independence. Although he appears to have no regrets about leaving his job, one senses he is not as satisfied as he claims. Even though he quit eventually, he worked for eight months after winning. It is the absence of some focused activity to occupy his time and hands which he misses, and by his own admission he is a loner.

"I don't have any close friends, at least none that I can really put my finger on. Friends are few and far between. You don't have many friends in a lifetime. You have a lot of acquaintances but no friends. There's a lot of fair-weather friends. A lot of people that never wanted to know me want to now. Loads of them. I had two women come up to me one day at the racetrack. They said they had the same name and they wanted to know if we were any relation. I didn't pay any attention to them. Relation. Ha!

"You know, that day they named a race in our honor. My son brought $1,000 to bet. There was a horse with the same name as ours and he told me to put $100 on it, but I didn't. It won. We don't go to the track very often, but we do play a lot of bingo—several nights a week. Here and in Pennsylvania. We buy ten boards apiece and a stack of specials. They pay off better in Pennsylvania, but we usually lose—I'd say about $150 a week."

Have you had any problems with your relatives because of the money?

"Not hardly, outside of more demands. Two or three of them are constantly making demands for money when they run short—my brothers and kids. I can't support all these people. Even the U.S. government can't. I can loan you $100 and I'm a nice guy, but when I ask for it back I'm an SOB.

"You know, the best thing I like about this money is that I'm not tied down. Some people earn this kind of money but are tied down to their jobs or home. Not me. I can leave and come back anytime. I'd say our life is much better now. I do just about everything I like more often now than before. But I'm just an average guy. Shit! I could buy a $100,000 home, but for what? And pay $400 a month in taxes for what? To show off? I don't know where we're moving yet. Someday I'll find what I want, but right now I'm still looking for the right place."

Ed's search for new experiences, his moving and travel may be an attempt to fill the void formerly occupied by his job. His generous gifts and careless spending are perhaps symptomatic of a life molded by poverty and deprivation. Now he is able to buy the luxuries he always dreamed of, but he is unprepared to manage his finances, so he spends to impress others (as in his ostentatious gambling) or unwisely on a twenty-eight foot boat he is afraid to take away from the dock. There is a tinge of boredom in his life, too, but not enough to propel him back into the stultifying jobs which victimized his productive years. And, after all, why should he work for a few thousand dollars? A very rational decision for someone who is fighting the compulsion to work—to break the routine of a lifetime.

While Ed has been able to avoid returning to work, other winners have not. The habit of work is strong. From childhood we are socialized into the world of work; taught that it is something we are expected to do, that we should like it because it can be fulfilling. Unfortunately, most winners did not have psychologically stimulating jobs, and consequently viewed work primarily in economic terms. When their financial needs were met by their winnings, they no longer felt the pressure to continue. But the non-economic functions of work also bind us to it. It structures our lives and occupies our time, and some winners, such as Jimmy and Margaret Siciliano, found they could not easily sever the bonds.

The suspense about winning weighed heavily on the Sicilianos' minds that summer day four years ago as they sat in an auditorium at Rutgers University awaiting the outcome of the drawings. Jimmy kept reliving a daydream he had had shortly after learning he was in the finals.

"It happened at the shop one morning in Newark. I was shaving in a mirror and suddenly I saw myself back home. I remembered that I won the money and I was leaping in ten-foot jumps shouting 'I won the million! I won the million!' Then I snapped out of it and collapsed on the floor."

Despite this omen, they were jolted when they heard their names announced as the grand-prize winners. Margaret lurched forward and gashed her head on a chair. Jimmy was so overcome he had to be assisted to the stage by two men so he could accept the prize. But after they regained their composure, they adjusted to the celebrity status which Lady Luck conferred on them. Jimmy has appeared on five television shows and suffered through countless interviews. He is a funny, warm-hearted, lovable fellow who says what he thinks, frequently in a flamboyant, gesticulating manner.

The Sicilianos made good press because of their cavalier attitude toward life and their candid plans for the future.

"When I won," said Jimmy, "I held up my keys, waved them around my head, and told them I'd never go back to work. I swore the day I won I'd quit, and I did."

He had been a plumber for twenty-five years, and worked the last twelve for the same contractor.

"He was sorry to see me go. I was the only mechanic he had. I think he was upset, too, when I told people how little I had been making [$8,000]. They could see how little I got for the work I did compared to what he charged.

"I made Margaret quit, too. It wasn't right for her to work. People might start talking about how a rich man makes his wife work in a factory."

But eight months later they went back to work.

"I'd get dizzy sitting home looking at the walls. The ceiling would start going round and round. My wife never had a pimple on her body, but she broke out in a rash from doing nothing and being around the house. She had to go to a dermatologist."

Until a few months ago, when she had a cataract removed, Margaret worked the night shift on the assembly line in a local factory. "I always worked the night shift. That way I can do my chores and housework in the day. I enjoy working because you're more happy when you work. I feel good when I'm accomplishing something, and I'm more calm. I can tolerate more when I'm working. When you work, you appreciate your time together more. When you're home too much, it gets like a steady job you're not keen on."

Jimmy countered: "That goes both ways!"

Margaret planned to return to work shortly, but she would have to find a different job. While she was convalescing, the night shift was discontinued and she refuses to work days. But she was determined to continue working, especially after her nervous reaction to inactivity. Jimmy also felt he should remain active, but was less committed to a full-time job, and he admitted that plumbing was not his first love.

"I got into it by accident. After World War II, I signed up with the VA for on-the-job training. I wanted to be a carpenter, but they put me into training as a plumber. I never wanted it. I kept asking about the carpenter's training and they assured me that I was going to get it, to wait a little longer. When they finally told me they were going to put me into plumbing, I nearly went "blah" [he clutched his throat and motioned as if vomiting]. They said not to worry. 'As soon as there's an opening, we'll call you and put you into carpentry.' I waited twenty-five years for that call."

Through the years he worked hard for low pay and few fringe benefits. He will receive no pension for the quarter-century he labored. "My first boss gave me no paid holidays and no vacations, and I worked for him for six years. My last boss gave me one week paid vacation, which we spent at the Jersey shore."

Jimmy works part-time now. He claims the boredom was too much and so he resorted to the only thing he knew well —plumbing. He opened an electric sewer-and-drain-cleaning company, and now his chief complaint is that he does not have enough work.

"Business is very bad. I took in less than $1,500 last year. I work very little now—I guess you might say I'm semiretired. But I want to work. Working is good for your health. When you're home, you crawl the walls. You sleep late in the morning and get out of shape. That's what was happening to me after I quit. My nerves were bothering me. I was jumpy and short of breath. My doctor gave me some pills, but they didn't help. I was gaining weight, too. So I took up tennis, bowling, golf, and skiing. And I joined a health club. I went in recently for a complete physical. Afterward the doctor came in to see me and I was nervous about the results. He said the best advice he could give me was to 'get off your ass and get back to work!' "

Although Jimmy looks trim for a man of fifty-one, he still complains of not feeling "right." His "nerves" are bothering him, and he attributes this to insufficient work. In an effort to increase business, he advertises regularly in three newspapers, has put a notice in his church bulletin, and hired a telephone-answering service. "But it hasn't helped much. I wish I was going full-bloom with my business out there."

Although he acknowledges they are better off now, he contends they still have financial problems. "As far as security goes, we're much better. But my expenses are very high. This house eats up a lot. It cost $76,000."

The house is in a hilly, rural part of New Jersey. It is custom-built and adjoined by a large in-ground pool. The maintenance costs are much higher than those on their previous home, and monthly mortgage payments and taxes are $554.

"It's triple here what we were paying for gas and electric. Even in the summer. It costs a lot to run the filter for the pool. Where we used to live, it would cost us $45 a month for all our utilities. Even though we were making a lot less, we used to manage to save $100 a month from my take-home pay and now we can't even do that. Our other house was eighty years old. It was beautiful. Inside, it had big colonial beams running across the ceiling. After we bought it, we had $5 in our pockets, but we were really proud of our accomplishment. We both worked full-time then. We were always running out of money. I would borrow from my daughters. Now I give *them* money."

"I think we do things less now," said Margaret. "Before, we used to go to the shore—to Seaside Heights—every weekend. We used to have a great time, playing games and gambling. We'd spend all our money and come home broke. We'd win some prizes and have a lot of fun. We hardly ever go now."

They are very generous with their winnings, and routinely

devour their annual check. Although they have received four, they have little to show for them besides the house, and now Jimmy says he is becoming more careful about spending.

"I'm starting to take it easy. Boy, the checks are going like the wind. Don't ask me where it goes, but it goes. You just don't realize it. I had to borrow $7,000 last year from the bank because we ran out of money."

The Sicilianos have adopted a life-style which they feel befits their new financial status. Jimmy personifies the saying of Josh Billings: "Live within your income, even if you have to borrow money to do so." Not liking his work, he quit, and would not let Margaret continue. He quickly learned two things, however: life can be pretty boring without work, even dirty work, and he was not really a rich man. Though plumbing was abhorrent to him, he realized it was a marketable skill and the only one he had. From his remarks it is apparent that one of Jimmy's primary reasons for working is to obtain money to match his lavish spending needs. He is in an unfortunate predicament. Ill-prepared for his windfall, he spends extravagantly. Wanting more income, he turns to work, but dislikes his occupation and cannot bring himself to go back full-time. Working for someone else is, in his idealized conception, unbecoming a rich man, who must have his own business even when there is no demand for his services. So he languishes and bemoans the economy, takes medication for his "nervous condition," works out at the gym, and spends compulsively. He is caught in a vicious circle which may well find him facing an uncertain and insecure old age, dreading the day his installments end.

White-collar workers were also tied to their jobs for the economic rewards of work, and a majority of them quit, too. Frank Santorino, an erstwhile insurance agent, provides us with an interesting example of what such people may do when the pressure to work is removed. Frank, an affable fellow of forty-five, lives with his wife and two sons in an imposing split-level home in one of the most fashionable

communities in New Jersey. The first thing he did after winning was to buy this house. They had been living in a
crowded five-room apartment and were planning to move—
but a house like this, which cost over $100,000, was unthink-
able. The second thing he did was to ease out of his job.

Frank, like his father, had been a bricklayer. For twenty
years he worked outdoors and enjoyed it. Then, five years
ago, he developed severe pain in his right arm, a condition
commonly referred to as tennis elbow. At the time, he and
his brother were working together as mason subcontractors.

"My arm got so bad I couldn't even hold a trowel. Business
was no good, either, so I decided to give up masonry and start
selling insurance. A friend of mine talked me into it. He gave
me a super sales job. I thought I could do all right. I knew that
most new salesmen sell right away to all of their friends and
relatives and then run out of customers and have to quit.
That's why I purposely didn't sell to them in the beginning.
I went to phone directories and got lists of names and ad-
dresses from there. I went to town halls and looked at city
directories and got other data. You'd be amazed at the
amount of information they have on you that is public—
where you live, how much you pay in taxes, how many children you have. People would ask me, 'Where did you get that
information?' It's all public."

During the five years he sold insurance Frank never took
a vacation. He worked feverishly because his income de-
pended solely on commissions. "I worked seven days a week
in the beginning. Day and night. I'd put in around seventy
hours a week."

His wife recalled those times as being particularly onerous.
"We had no family life, no time to ourselves."

Frank was not happy with his work, either. He did not like
working indoors, but most of all he was distressed by the
financial problems of his potential clients.

"Selling insurance wasn't me. The most dissatisfying thing
about the job was when you knew people needed insurance
and couldn't afford it. Many's the premium I put out to help

them pay their first installment, especially after I won the money. But their first payment was often their last."

The empathy he had for his clients gnawed at him, and soon after he won he began reducing the hours he worked.

A month before I spoke with him, he quit. Though presently unemployed, he is optimistic about the future. Following several unsuccessful encounters with doctors, he tried acupuncture. After five treatments he experienced a remission of the pain, and the strength returned to his arm. Now he is bowling again and has a 180 average. He is also active around the house, repairing and remodeling.

"I help my neighbors with this, too. I can't stand still. I'm too young to retire and sit around. I have a lot of nervous energy. Actually, I'd like to go back to bricklaying. I'm thinking of forming a construction company and bringing my sons into it, but the construction industry isn't in good shape right now."

Since they had no cash from the sale of a previous house, the down payment on their home and the remodeling have claimed much of the four checks they have received.

"It costs me three times more to live here than what it did before. We used to live on $12,000 to $13,000 a year. After the mortgage and the taxes, there really isn't too much to invest—maybe $8,000 to $10,000. There's not much you can do with that, really. It's the old story. You always spend whatever your income is. People think you're a millionaire, but it's a fictitious title. You get $50,000 a year and a lot of that is taxed. [His taxes have been averaging about $20,000 a year.] My definition of a millionaire is someone who can go out and spend all he wants, and none of us can do that."

Frank quit masonry because of his health and turned to a white-collar job, the kind of work many parents want for their children: clean, indoors, working with one's head instead of one's hands, at a desk instead of in a trench. But the veneer of his new occupation quickly wore off and exposed the long hours, relatively low pay, and the problems of insecure, disadvantaged people. It was too much for him, and he got out. Despite his rehabilitation and professed desire to return to masonry, he has not taken the jump back into the ranks of the employed. He keeps himself occupied around the house and helps neighbors with repairs, but does not want to work for someone else. Just as Jimmy wanted his own business, Frank is considering starting a construction company, but he is more prudent, awaiting a favorable economic climate. Once the economic chain shackling us to our jobs is broken, there may be a longing for activity, but apparently heretofore stable working people are able to endure the state of unemployment, at least for several years, if there is an alternative source of income.

While Frank was openly disenchanted with white-collar salesmanship, other white-collar workers, like Ike and Shirley Pleskowicz, ostensibly liked their jobs, but quit nevertheless. Ike is fifty-one and Shirley forty-eight. Four years have passed since they won. They still live in Philadelphia on a street lined with rows of aging duplexes. One can tell the houses apart only by their numbers. Block after block, row after row, they stand like army barracks. There are few trees and no green yards. Concrete driveways fill the space between houses. The little grass on the lawns is brown. It was a windy day when I called, and blowing papers were collecting in front of house steps, trapped by the bordering hedges.

Despite the sterile appearance of the area, there was a sense of community, of belongingness, among the residents, and that is why the Pleskowiczs have remained. They have lived here for eighteen years.

"We raised our children here," said Ike. "I used to come home from work and find Billy playing under those stairs. Sometimes I'd think it was him but it was a friend. He'd be outside in the back playing, while his friends would be in here. There were lots of kids for him to play with. That's his school back there. That big brick building. And there's our church. They're all right nearby. There are all kinds of people here—Polish, Italian, Irish."

Another reason they had not moved was Shirley's mother.

"My mother lived with us from the time we were married—twenty-six years," said Shirley. "She was an invalid. She had arthritis and in her last few years developed cancer. For the last two years she was very ill, and I cared for her here until she died. I wouldn't think of putting her in a home, which we might have had to do if we had moved.

"We come from a working class," Shirley said sternly. "My father was a baker and Ike's father was a steel worker. We were never afraid to work. Work is work. We were brought up from stock that said, 'Don't be afraid to work, and working with your hands is all right.' "

Yet, neither of you works now. What did you do, Shirley?

"I was an accountant technician for the government for fourteen years. I did bookkeeping and checked other people's work when there was trouble."

"I worked as an electronics-equipment specialist for the Navy," added Ike. "It was a Civil Service job. I was in procurement and logistics. I had to make sure that the right amount of parts and equipment were on hand to service and resupply the planes. I was responsible for procuring and providing parts for nine thousand Navy aircraft. We had to keep them flying.

"I was there nineteen years. I only had a high-school education. I wasn't going to move very far, so I decided to take up their offer and went into training to be an electronics specialist. I started when I was thirty-five. It lasted for four years. It's kind of rough when you're out of school for eighteen years. I had to go through all forms of math and physics. You're sitting there and look around and see eighteen- and nineteen-year-olds and ask yourself, 'What the hell are *you* doing here, old man?' I burned the midnight oil a lot. But I got through and got my state license as an electronics specialist."

"I was real proud of him, knowing that he did well. He started at Civil Service grade seven and ended at eleven," said Shirley.

"That's right. I made two double grade jumps in two years.

I was the only man to do this in my outfit in twenty-eight years. I never even put in for them. My boss came up and said, 'You just been jumped two grades!' A year later to the day, he did the same thing."

Did you like your job?

"We were both very satisfied with our jobs," said Shirley. "I worked for the Army and I know that people worked hard there and enjoyed it. We weren't like what people think about 'typical' government workers. You can't give labels to people. We worked hard."

"It's like any job," Ike said. "You see guys collecting garbage outside. One guy empties four cans in the same amount of time another guy will do one."

Shirley could not think of anything that was dissatisfying about her job. "I was in a spot that I liked. We didn't even use our sick leave. If you don't feel good, I figure you should go in anyway. You feel better. It's therapy. Yes, work is therapy. It occupies your mind."

What is the important thing about having a job?

"Doing it well."

Ike interrupted: "That's right, and having the satisfaction that it was done well."

She continued: "Because if it wasn't done well, you come home and ask yourself why."

Did your jobs give you a chance to make decisions?

"They encouraged it," said Shirley.

"At times certain tasks were routine," said Ike, "but others you could be creative in. The only thing that dissatisfied me was when you think things were working out right and the human element loused up the whole thing. You'd set it all up and find out later somebody did something wrong down the line.

"You know what used to burn me up? When someone would come over at the end of the day and ask, 'How much did you do today?' Never 'How much *good* did you do today?' I would pull out a sheet of problems that haven't been solved in twenty years and say, 'Look at these questions. They've been around for twenty years. I've been here only two."

How much were you making in your jobs?

Shirley: "I was making about $10,000 a year."

Ike: "I made $16,000 a year."

You were making good money and you both say you liked your work. Why did you quit?

"I kept working for two years after I won," said Ike. "Then I left. I used to travel a lot and I figured why should I put up with all the aggravation for $1 or $1.50 an hour? That's about what it would be after taxes. I pay all kinds of taxes on the money. Federal tax, state tax, and city tax. The state and city tax alone run $2,000 a year. And, believe it or not, some people don't want you to work. They didn't needle me, but you could feel it in the air—the tension."

"I never went back," said Shirley, "except two weeks later to hand in my resignation, and at that time I gave my friend at work who sold me the ticket $2,000. She never asked for it. She thanked me. I wanted to stay. I loved my work. But I had my mother to care for and I was afraid it would be hard on me if I went back."

"I know she was a good worker," interjected Ike. "They would have shown her no mercy."

"My supervisors called me up and told me to think about it and come back. They liked my work. But where I worked they were forever having rifts and laying people off. You were unsure of your position. I went to work for the money. If you don't need it and don't have to fight over it anymore, why take it away from someone else?

"Until my mother died, I was caring for her. She was very ill the last two years. Ike spends much of his time around the house. He's very handy. He fixes things up."

"That's right. I did the wallpapering in there, and I paint, too."

They feel obliged to remain here until Billy finishes college. "When he gets out on weekends, he still feels this is his home," Ike said proudly.

"I'm responsible for my children," said Shirley. "I hope

they don't have any hardships and have a good life. The only change since we won is you feel if you want to get something you're not strapped. You can buy new things, but I feel basically, inside, a person doesn't change. You want to be liked for what you are."

Ike and Shirley present us with some puzzling contrasts. Their comments reflect the work ethic with its emphasis on initiative and industriousness. They professed a strong affinity for their jobs and displayed pride in their accomplishments. Their salaries were adequate, and they enjoyed good working conditions and fringe benefits. Their remarks revealed important values which work provided them. They prized it as an important factor in their lives; it kept them busy and, they assumed, healthy. They also viewed work as a morally correct activity—something they were supposed to do. One does not shy away from work, but welcomes it. "We come from a working class . . . we were never afraid to work." Finally, and most important, they valued work for the money.

They instilled their sense of reverence for work in their children and were proud that the children respected and emulated them. Ike and Shirley gave them love and affection but virtually no money from the winnings lest it corrupt them. The two driving forces in their lives were their children and Shirley's mother. The passing of her mother and the maturation of their children created a void. Their new financial security meant that the economic necessity for working was also removed. The purposes that work served were suddenly unimportant. The troublesome aspects of their jobs were now magnified. We hear of Shirley's disgust over the petty infighting among co-workers, and Ike's frustration with incompetent colleagues who misunderstood his intentions and destroyed his projects. We learn, too, how they carried their complaints home with them. Winning removed the necessity for tolerating this situation. Despite recognition for his accomplishments, Ike quit. Although Shirley moralistically praised the virtues of work, she never returned. Their actions belie their attitudes and expose the tenuous link between what people say and what they do. Their major problem was not quitting but justifying their actions to themselves and their children, so they might reconcile the conflict between their behavior and their values. The emphasis on anticipated harassment from Shirley's coworkers and Ike's exaggeration of his income-tax responsibilities seem rationalizations for not working.

Shirley had been unemployed for four years, but until recently was deeply involved in caring for her dying mother. Ike had not worked in the last two years. Now that the children are on their own and Shirley's mother is gone, they are beginning to look to the future. They have bought a house at the Jersey shore, are thinking about moving and, perhaps, even going back to work. But their plans are tentative. Shirley seemed resigned and complacent about her new status, but Ike was restless. He groped for an answer to a question about his future activities and admitted, "I will have to find something." Clearly he was bored but unable or unwilling to overcome his inertia.

Job satisfaction and work commitment are intangible phenomena—difficult to assess because what people say and what they do are often at variance. Moreover, social and economic pressures force us to say and do things we might not intend, or repeat under different circumstances. The freedom to act, to choose between working and not working, is seldom available to us, making questions based upon people's attitudes about this question irrelevant if not absurd.

But we have seen a pervasive one-dimensional work-orientation among the winners. They viewed work instrumentally, as a means to an end. When they achieved economic independence, they quit their jobs. In reviewing their comments and experiences, one is struck by the lack of commitment to their jobs these people manifested. A variety of rationalizations were given to justify quitting, such as the remark of a friend or co-worker, in some instances even the suspicion that people's attitudes toward them might change.

What stands out from the interviews is that many people, when given an opportunity to choose between keeping their jobs and quitting, chose the latter. The primary reasons for working in the United States are survival and habit. The experience of these winners indicates that once people's survival needs are met, the habit of working in their present jobs can be broken. When these people had a chance, they knew what to do—they got out. This break had serious social and psychological ramifications. Some people were unable to cope with their unemployed status. After a lifetime of structured activity, they did not know how to fill their hours and exchanged the tension and toil of their jobs for boredom and monotony in their expensive new homes.

Even when they want to return to work, the lottery winners are frustrated. Since many lack marketable skills, the awareness of broader horizons, and the perspicacity for innovative investments, they are put into a conflictive situation. They are loath to return to their old jobs or similar undesirable ones, but they are socially, occupationally, and psychologically unprepared for more challenging types of work. Hence, they sit at home and while away the hours. Many winners admitted they were looking for something to do, but the prospects of finding dream jobs are not good. They are victims of their lack of education and training. Before, they were unable to attain financial security. Now they are unprepared to cope with it. A cruel prank of Lady Luck.

CHAPTER 5

Longing to Share,
But Nobody's There: The Widows

"There are few sorrows, however poignant,
in which a good income is of no avail."
—LOGAN PEARSALL SMITH

Charlotte Dubowski, a seventy-year-old widow, has lived all her life in a workingclass suburb of Buffalo. Her son and his family reside in her aging two-story house within earshot of the roar of jets at Buffalo International Airport. She spends almost all her time at home watching television because she has multiple debilitating health problems. Her breathing is labored, and she is afflicted with arteriosclerosis. Her last job was in 1956 as a furniture sewer in a nearby factory; she was forced to leave because of her failing health.

For years Charlotte looked forward to her weekly shopping trip to a local market and to Sunday church services. These were her only opportunities to escape from her house, except for occasional meetings with an old friend, Jimmy Callahan. At the market, she would purchase two lottery tickets, one for herself and one for Jimmy. Six years ago one of these brought her $50,000, which she split with him. She spent a few hundred dollars on a new washer and dryer, and then made elaborate plans for her first vacation in years that summer with Jimmy. But this was not to be—four months later he died. Her health has steadily deteriorated since then, and the money remains in the bank for her declining years.

A lottery windfall would seem to be a primary ingredient in the recipe of happiness, but, as Mark Twain once said, "To get the full value of a joy, you must have somebody to share it with." The truth of this statement is vividly depicted in the following stories of widows. Although they are now financially secure, they have mixed feelings about winning. As one put it, "I have good days and bad days." The joy of winning has not filled the void in their lives. Even those no longer grieving reflect occasionally on the hardships they once endured and lament that their husbands are not able to share the good times, too. For most, there is a sense of loneliness, a hollowness to their joy. They are, like Doris Turner, at once elated and forlorn.

Doris won a million dollars three years ago, just ten months after her husband died. She is forty-six and lives in a remote corner of New Jersey. Her house is situated on a wooded three-acre lot. The rooms—there are ten—are spacious and filled with beautiful furniture. The living room has a cathedral ceiling, and an immense fireplace occupies an entire wall. "Years ago my husband and I would go for rides in this area. I always wanted to live here. When I won, I started looking and found this."

The house cost $118,000, and its $80,000 mortgage requires monthly payments of $500. In addition, the property taxes run $3,000 a year. The $8,000 she spent for furniture, plus the Plymouth Satellite and Toyota she bought for her sons, exhausted her first installments. "I was hoping to sell the old house and use that for the down payment, but the market fell apart. I was asking $41,000 for it, but I'm willing to take less." She was eagerly awaiting her third check at the end of the week.

Doris is beginning to think about investing, but admits she does not know what to do. "I'm not a social person, so I don't get much advice on investing. I'm scared stiff. I hope I don't blow it on a bad investment. That's why I got this house. In case something happened, the kids would have it."

She has a large responsibility, supporting four sons. She put two through college, and another is about to enter. Although she gets $500 a month from Social Security, within two years three of the boys will no longer qualify as dependents. The winnings however, have opened up new options. Doris believes in being active and utilizing her potentialities. A year and a half before she won, she decided to get a job.

"I wanted to have something to do. My kids were older. How many dishes can you clean? How many walls can you scrub? So I went to work. I started working in a large factory and was there for several months when the shop steward told me that they were going to lay off some people. I had more seniority than some others and he said he would bump another woman out of a job who had less than me. I talked it over with my husband. He was a shop steward at another factory. I felt bad about putting someone out of a job, but he told me it was a common practice and I had every right to do it. I went to my steward and said I wanted to stay. Then I asked who I would be bumping, and it was a girlfriend. But I found out that I had more seniority than a man in a clerking position, so I said I wanted that job. The union backed me up, even though no woman ever worked in that department before.

"The job was as a stockroom clerk. I kept the cardex records. Any high-school idiot could do it, but it kept me on my toes—the little battle that went on there. They didn't like having me there, but I did my work well. My job didn't require me to talk with anyone, and they kept it that way. Some of the men used to bait the supervisor, but I didn't get into that. When my husband died, the flak calmed down, but I resented why they stopped. They felt sorry for me as a widow, not as a fellow worker.

"I didn't expect to move up in that job. There was nowhere I could go under the circumstances. There was no way I could make supervisor. But I hoped to get a raise. Then I won the money. They started giving me funny flak. You know, like 'Here comes Miss Money Bags.' I was trying desperately to make the second anniversary to see if I'd get my raise. I was in line for a good one, but I couldn't hold out any longer. Every day the boss would ask, 'Have you made your mind up yet?' So I finally told him what he wanted to hear. After I left, they dissolved the job because another woman was ready to move into it."

Doris was unemployed for about a year and a half. Two months ago she obtained a part-time job in a craft shop specializing in needlepoint. There she sells and teaches, and seems satisfied.

"I'm working, but not for the money—for something interesting to do and to get the experience in customer relations. Working is important for your general well-being and self-satisfaction. It gives me a chance to get out into the world—into the mainstream of things. The only way I can stay in life is to get out there and work. I always wanted to do this kind of work. I like the artistic part of it and meeting people. I waited to find a job like this for a long time."

Confident of her potential, she hopes to open a needlecraft shop of her own someday. Until then she is content to remain where she is, learning and developing her skills. Although her outlook on life has been improving, she wishes her husband were here to enjoy the winnings. She recalled the day she won:

"When the serial number came out for the final drawing, it was on my son's birthday. I knew I was going to win. I took three of my boys with me to the drawing. I told the boss I'd like to be there for it. 'If I'm going to win, I want to bring it home myself.' He just laughed. I said I was serious, that I *was* going to win.

"The day I won was one of mixed feelings. I was crying when I went up there. One of the newspapers showed a picture of me like this and it had the caption 'Agonizing Joy.' That pretty well summed up the way I really felt.

"At the drawing they were playing 'Spanish Eyes.' My kids used to play that in their rock group. Then the band began to play 'Put Your Head on My Shoulder.' I turned to one of my sons and said, 'Aren't those beautiful words?' I felt very nostalgic and started to cry a little. I felt my husband was with us that day."

The joy of winning may be accompanied by a sense of helplessness and confusion. Widows frequently have questions about what to do with the money and how to protect it. Many, like Helga Fischer, were unprepared to cope with the financial problems because their husbands had controlled the family finances.

Helga is seventy-four years old. She lives in a quaint section of a New Jersey town where the homes are meticulously kept. The lawns are neatly manicured and bordered by shrubs and trees. It is as if a little New England community had been transplanted there. Helga has lived in her house for thirty-five years.

"My husband built a lot of it," she said with a distinctive German accent. "He died about a year ago, but I can't leave here. I guess I'm too sentimental, and where would I go? Wherever I'd move, I'd be a stranger."

She has thought about moving because of all the notoriety she received after winning a million dollars six months ago.

"I never thought I would win. Never. I didn't even go to the drawing. Then I got a call from Trenton. I thought it was a joke. They told me again and I couldn't even talk, I was so upset. A little later two policemen came to the door. They asked if I was the lady who won a million dollars. I told them yes and they came in. They were called by the people in Trenton. They told them that I sounded very upset on the phone and they came to see if I was all right. Then the phone started to ring. It's a good thing they were there. They took the calls for me. I wanted to have the phone disconnected, but it was a weekend and they couldn't do it until Tuesday. The police took care of it for me. The papers and television wanted to interview me, but I said no interviews. But the next day they had my name in all the local papers—even the *Daily News*—and even my address."

The shock of winning was too much for her. Just ten months before, her husband had died after a long illness. He was seventy-five and had been retired for ten years from his job as chief electrician in an ice-cream plant, where he had worked for thirty years. They had no children during their forty-five years of marriage. The blow of his death precipitated a serious stomach ailment for Helga that has left her somewhat incapacitated. "The doctor told me to stay in. I never set a foot out of the house after my husband died."

She has not yet recovered from the shock of winning. Initially, she was reluctant to speak. We conversed through a glass storm door, and she was visibly disturbed when I mentioned the lottery. Even after I established some rapport and was invited in, she would periodically take off her glasses and massage her eyes to brush back tears.

"You can't imagine the problems I had. All the trouble it's caused me. It wasn't worth it."

You really think you'd be better off without it?

"No, don't get me wrong. Not in that way. It has helped. I would have lost the house. We lived here for thirty-five years, but it's old and needs repairs. My husband only had a small pension. As soon as he closed his eyes, that stopped. I get Social Security and that's all. They just reassessed our taxes and doubled them. They're $1,000 a year. And the back [of the house] was falling in. That's going to cost $5,000. The materials are in the garage. It needs to be painted, too. I just couldn't have kept it."

Did you get a lot of letters?

"Yes. One was funny. It was from a German woman in Elizabeth. She said, 'Since you're probably going to be giving money away anyway, why not give me $3,000–4,000.' Another one came from a young girl who wanted me to give her $5,000 so she could give it to her parents so they could take trips."

Do you still buy lottery tickets?

"No. I only used to buy two a week. One for my husband and one for me. I wish I could have shared it all with him—

that he was here. He would have gotten a laugh out of it all. Instead, I was all alone. I can't even go out of the house. I don't have a car, because I can't drive. I haven't spent much because my lawyer told me to go slow. Anyway, what can a seventy-four-year-old woman who isn't healthy do? I thought about taking a trip, but I can't get around. My nephew helps me a lot. He lives near me and he comes over. He helped me during all the trouble, too.

"I can't spend the money because I stay in, and taxes take about half, and I can't leave it either. My lawyer told me I won't be able to give it away because of the taxes. He didn't know what to do. He said it's never happened before, but after I go they can't settle the estate for twenty years. I don't even have a chance to spend the money, and I can't give it all away, and I'm seventy-four. They ought to do something about that."

A marked fear of strangers is often evinced by elderly widows like Helga. Actually, this may be a beneficial reaction, because many of them are vulnerable. But widows like Helga were grateful for winning. The lottery snatched them from the grip of poverty, gave them hope and a new lease on life.

To Rita Fortunato, the money forestalled financial disaster, but she has had to pay a high price to avoid it. They say there is a silver lining in every cloud, and so, too, misfortune sometimes accompanies Lady Luck. On the day Rita left for the drawing, her husband became ill. "I went to Atlantic City for the drawing and he got sick and went to bed." Rita won $200,000 ($20,000 for ten years), but her sixty-seven-year-old husband never shared it with her. He died two months later. "We were hoping to go on a cruise, but he never got better."

At fifty-nine, she is attractive and energetic, and has assumed full command of their Italian restaurant, where she works six days a week from eleven A.M. to eleven P.M., managing, supervising thirty-three employees, and cashiering. I interviewed her in the restaurant during working hours. She was bouncing up and down, giving advice, and taking cash and phone calls during our three-hour conversation. She enjoys her work, especially since it gives her a chance to be active and meet people. The Fortunatos opened the restaurant thirty-four years ago, right after they were married. Six months later Rita's husband was drafted into World War II. She dutifully took control, working feverishly to keep the business going. "I would open up the place at eight A.M. and close the bar at two or three in the morning."

The building is 115 years old, but you would never know it. It is immaculately kept, and the appointments are adequate—even a bit on the posh side in the addition Rita built with some of the winnings. But, despite the fine food and accommodations, the business is not doing well.

"Things are very slow. It's off forty percent this year over last. There's no money around. Inflation is hurting us. The bills keep coming: food, heat, electricity. Inflation increases my bills, but I can't raise the cost of the food. Most of the people we serve are families. They come in two or three times a week. We have lots of regular customers. If we raised the cost of our food, we'd lose them."

Rita has had to put large sums into the business to keep it going. In three years she plowed in half her winnings ($30,000).

"If it hadn't been for the winnings, I probably would have sold the place. Before I won, things were good. There was plenty of money around. People were spending. I was drawing $200 a week salary from it, but I've had to stop this now. I'm staying here because my bookkeeper and lawyer told me if I sold it now I wouldn't get what I had invested in it. So I'll keep it until I can get what I want for it." (She estimated the value of the restaurant at $500,000.)

Rita works hard and derives satisfaction from being able to keep the business going. "It's the idea that I was able to run it. The pleasure of running it smooth all the way around. The work isn't easy. I have to think about the worrying and do the sales tax. I don't think you can ever learn enough. I've been doing it for thirty-four years and I learn something new every day."

But the demands of the business restrict her outside activities. "There's no family life. Just work, work, work. You're a slave to the place. You have no time to enjoy yourself. It's like working a double shift, and you make the same money, except you're your own boss."

Despite her busy schedule, Rita is able to accomplish her errands on her day off, Monday. She rarely goes out or has time for common leisure activities like movies, entertaining, and visiting, and has had only three vacations in recent years. The year before last, she closed the restaurant for three weeks while the addition was being built. She did not go away because she was needed to advise the builders. Last year she again closed the restaurant for two weeks. Both times she used some of the winnings to give her employees two weeks' paid vacation.

Rita spends little of the winnings on herself. She took a brief cruise with her mother to the Bahamas, and bought a $10,000 crypt for her husband, with ten family plots which she had to purchase to get the crypt. About a third of her winnings have gone into bank savings certificates.

Since she was an early winner, she received an inordinate number of harassing calls and letters. "Oh, my God, it was terrible! I got letters from all over New York. One man said he had plenty to eat, so he just wanted a little a week to live on. Another man called at two A.M. He said he needed money for his house closing the next morning. I said, 'Do you know what time it is?' and he said, 'That's all right, I'll be right over.'"

The phone calls and mail were not her only problems. Her house was broken into twice in the three weeks after she won. "One night we came home and found a man on the porch. My son and son-in-law chased him, but he got away. He got into a car that was waiting for him. They followed the car and got its license number. Trenton checked it and found that the car was stolen. Nothing was taken from the house, but my jewelry box was opened and on the floor. He must have dropped it when we surprised him by coming home early."

This experience impelled her to install a burglar alarm and fence. She also got an unlisted phone number, and has not been bothered since.

Knowing she has money to keep the business afloat is not reassuring, because she would like to save for her retirement. Although she has no specific plans for future installments, she knows what she would not like to do with them. "I'm only hoping that it doesn't go in here."

In contrast to Rita's active outgoing life-style is the more sheltered life of Alice Bowers.

Alice, in her late forties, was working as a waitress not far from her home. She didn't expect her life to change much from her normal routine until that fateful day, four years ago, when she won a million dollars. She was in the crowd, waiting to see if she would carry away some prize money, but never expected to hit the jackpot. When her name was announced, she was so overcome with emotion that a nurse went to her aid and she had to be assisted onto the stage.

Alice's friends in the Millionaire's Club refer to her as outgoing, gregarious, and jovial, but when I interviewed her she seemed fearful and suspicious. She greeted me at the door wearing a white housecoat. It was 11:30 in the morning. Although it was bitter cold and a sharp wind whistled down the bleak city street where her small one-family house was situated, she did not invite me in. Instead, I conducted the interview through a storm door.

Alice has been unemployed for four years. She wanted to continue working, but "The other waitresses got jealous. There was too much pressure, so I had to quit. I worked there for seven years before, and I liked the job."

There were other problems, too. Some of her in-laws no longer speak to her because she didn't give them as much as they wanted. She has no children, and this rejection further isolated her. However, she is not completely alone. Her sister-in-law, who quit her job as a high-school nutritionist, lives with her, and together they exist on the installments. They do not live extravagantly. There were no new cars, expensive clothes, or exotic trips. Most of the money is banked each year. As I thanked Alice for cooperating and bade her farewell, her final comment was: "It's all right as long as it doesn't get into the papers. There are a lot of nasty people around here—in the projects."

The shock of winning and its aftermath can even cause physiological problems. Minnie Petraglia, fifty-eight, was in poor health before she won a million dollars four years ago, and the strain of winning threatened to tip the scales against her. She is a timid, frail person. When she won, she was trying to eke out a living for herself and her youngest daughter by working part-time at a local supermarket.

Interviewing Minnie was difficult because her children tried to insulate her from anxieties which might exacerbate her infirmities. When I finally managed to locate her apartment, two young men angrily met me at the door.

I explained my purpose, but they seemed hostile.

"She doesn't want to speak with you. No interviews. She doesn't want to give any interviews," said a dark six-footer becoming increasingly annoyed. The other young man interjected: "You must know how it is. All the trouble she's had. All the publicity."

This gave me an opportunity to drop a few names and experiences of other winners, and the atmosphere became less tense. Minnie and a young woman moved into the room, offered me a seat, and introduced the others. The tall, dark fellow was her son, Jeffrey, the woman was her daughter, Phyllis, and the other young man was her son-in-law, Bob.

Did you have any really bad experiences?

"Not really. I got lots of letters from all over the world. Most of them weren't even in English. They came from Spain, Africa, India, Italy, Germany. I got lots of proposals, too."

Jeffrey interrupted: "Yeah, from men who thought, 'Here's an old widow. . . .'"

Minnie continued: "I had one of the letters translated by a friend. It came from Spain. It was from a man who said he was very good-looking and wanted to get to know me. A lot of the letters came right to where I worked at the supermarket. My boss told me they came every day, but he didn't give them to me. He said they were just nuisances or were very sad. 'I don't think you'd like to read them. I throw them out.'

"And, you know, I get all kinds of advice. People say to me, 'If I had the money, I'd do this and I'd do that.'

"I like to play bingo, but a lot of people resent me being there. Even a friend of mine acted that way. One night, right at the bingo table, she came up and said, 'What the hell are you doing here? Let someone else win. You don't need the money.' She wasn't kidding, either. I almost cried. I went to bingo not for money but because it was my only chance to get out of the house.

"Even my younger daughter had problems. She would come home from school in tears. 'I can't even go to school. Kids come up and tell me to give them a quarter, give them a dollar.' She's such a generous person. I told her, 'From now on, don't take money to school with you.' She was getting to the point where she didn't know who her friends were."

How about work? What happened there?

"So many people came to see me at work. It was such an annoyance. That was one of the reasons I left my job. I was heartbroken. I loved my work, really, but the main reason I left was because of my health. The year before I won and after it, I was in the hospital four times. I had three heart attacks and a stroke. I was in and out of the hospital. I couldn't work anymore."

"I think the stress of winning might have affected her health, too," said Jeffrey. "She worried a lot, especially about the publicity and her grandchildren. She was afraid for them. A lot of people don't know how to handle it. Some are open and know what to do and some are afraid of it more, like in her case. She was so afraid, she was even afraid she was going to win!"

"It does scare you," said Minnie. "I couldn't imagine myself winning. The day I found out I was in the finals I just came home from the hospital after a heart attack, and I was looking at the doctor and hospital bills and wondering how I was going to pay them."

What do you do with the money?

"I give a lot to my children, and I paid for my youngest daughter's wedding. Our life was always hard. My husband was a truckdriver and we always struggled. He worked hard all his life. He stayed away a lot to make ends meet, and he died when he was forty-seven. We were never able to get lots of things for our children, like the toys I wanted them to have. When I won, I wanted to share with them my happiness, because I couldn't when they were younger."

"What do you mean never had anything?" said Phyllis. "We got more love and affection than anyone could ask for."

"I don't save much now," said Minnie. "I have about $5,-000 in stock, but really I spend it all and give it away to my kids."

"And that's fine," said Jeffrey. "That's what I think she should be doing at her age. Using it and having a good time. She's more secure now. There's less tension. Her health has been better now after the first few months. I think many times how it has kept her alive."

"I'm happy," said Minnie. "I spend more time with my grandchildren now. I was working part-time before and I liked my job and my boss liked my work, but he asked me to put in more time or he'd have to get someone who could work more. So I worked more to keep my job, and the government took back two of my Social Security checks. I planned to work full-time after my daughter turned eighteen if my health stayed up. I wanted to be self-sufficient. I didn't want to take anything away from my children; they had their own problems. Jeff has four children of his own to support. I don't knock the lottery. It's a wonderful thing. It's a godsend. Without that, I wouldn't be able to manage."

Once Minnie was able to obtain a degree of privacy and security, the money proved to have a salutary effect on her. In time, most widows made the transition, as they had when they lost their husbands. Yet the wound from the loss of a loved one is deep, and even outgoing, mirth-loving people such as Wilma Kovaleski were unable to hide the scars completely.

Wilma, sixty-two, won a million dollars two years ago. She is a buxom blonde, amiable and quick-witted, and a bit of a celebrity. In addition to numerous newspaper interviews, she appeared on the nationally televised programs *To Tell the Truth* and the *David Susskind Show*. We met for lunch at a restaurant on the Jersey coast, and I began our conversation by asking whether her life had changed.

"No, I wouldn't say so. I'm just doing what I used to, except more of it." The "more of it" refers to her expanded travel itinerary, which includes recent trips to San Francisco and South America. Actually, her life has changed quite a bit. Before she won, she was forced to live modestly on her $6,400 court-clerk's salary and dividends from stock her husband left. He was a business agent in the Teamsters Union and had been making about $400 a week. When he died many years ago, Wilma had to readjust her life-style. To make ends meet, in addition to her regular job, she clerked part-time in two other courts. Then in 1966 she suffered a stroke which partially paralyzed her right side. The effects of this are almost gone, although she does have a slight limp. This is complicated by a weight problem, for which she takes medication.

"The doctor wants me to lose a hundred pounds. I've lost twenty so far. I've been thinking about going to Duke to take their special diet. I think it will run about $10,000."

But her life is much better now.

"I don't have to worry about money. Before, I was pressed. My daughter and her husband, who was unemployed at the time, were living with me. I had to take money out of the savings bank regularly to make it. I had even spoken with a real-estate agent about listing my house."

Wilma does not work anymore. She wanted to retire immediately after winning, but was persuaded to stay on and train her successor. This period lasted five months. She now collects $30 a month from her Civil Service pension and $200 a month from Social Security.

"I was scared at first, so I had my sons live with me for a week. My phone is unlisted—it was before I won, so that was no problem, but I did get a lot of mail. I got letters from every state but Alaska. Twenty-four in one day."

In addition to traveling, she spent a considerable sum on remodeling her house of nineteen years, including flood-lights to illuminate the grounds and discourage intruders. She does not want to move—"I have many good friends here"—though one of her neighbors took exception to the lights. She had to go to court because of it and is now constructing an eight-foot fence to block the light—and the neighbors.

She has also bought new clothes, some finer paintings than she was able to afford before, jewelry, and a silver Continental Mark IV. After paying her average yearly $18,000 tax bill, she gives $3,000 a year to each of her three children. She also gave $2,000 to an old girlfriend living in the Midwest, and various amounts to charities and churches. Wilma estimates she gives away between $12,000 and $13,000 annually. She has also purchased some saving certificates as investments.

Wilma is religious and attends church regularly, but admits, "The way they've changed it [Roman Catholicism], it's very confusing, but I believe in God. He wanted me to have this money—I believe He had a hand in it."

In speaking with her, you know she is happy. As she puts it, "I'm a pretty contented person." This is reflected in her generosity. She does not desire great wealth and, indeed, may not know how to spend all she has. Nevertheless, she still purchases lottery tickets and emphatically states, "I'm gonna do it again!"

The last time we spoke together, we were at her house thumbing through her scrapbook on the lottery when a small piece of paper fell out on the table. It was a melancholy poem about the loss of a loved one. "I cut it out of a magazine after

I won," she said in uncharacteristic solemnity, "because it reminded me of my husband."

Angela D'Antonio's story is a case of dreams never realized because of the death of a loved one, but there is a happy ending. Angela worked for thirty years in the Internal Revenue Service and looked forward to her retirement, when she and her husband would be able to do the things they had always dreamed of.

"For twenty years we lived a very quiet life. I commuted to the city every day and went to bed at ten o'clock. We would spend two weeks at the Catskills each summer and two weeks at the shore. My husband had worked forty-one years at A&P, and he was waiting a little bit longer for his retirement. We had a perfect plan all set up, and then he died. I went on working because I loved it. Being a tax examiner was a marvelous job. The IRS and all the people were wonderful to work for, too. I was a fast worker. I could do the work of three people. After ten years I was getting up there in money and I never asked for a promotion. I even turned them down twice because I didn't want to earn more than my husband. I dealt mainly with tax-collecting and tax preparation and I was responsible for interviewing people in an attempt to collect delinquent accounts. I also prepared financial statements and initiated distraint actions when necessary. The girls used to tease me and say, 'How could you like it?' I guess I was one of the few crazy ones who enjoyed it.

"After my husband died, I transferred to an office closer to my home, and I worked as a taxpayer service representative. I assisted people in preparing their federal income-tax returns, and I advised them on the regulations. I had to interpret Internal Revenue laws, practices, rulings, and procedures. This new job began to get me down, especially during the big drive around tax time. The four phones would be ringing at the same time. I'd talk to fifty, seventy people a day. Things were very hectic. People would be arguing all the time. Some were really mean—like I was personally to blame for their problems. Many were senior citizens and felt they shouldn't have to pay taxes. A colored woman even threw her bag at me one day.

"One interesting thing happened. From time to time, a person would come in to ask advice about taxes because they had won the lottery. I started seeing these $50,000 checks coming across my desk and began wondering about it. I didn't know much about the lottery. I was brought up so strictly in the IRS. You couldn't gamble. A lot of agents were fired for buying Irish Sweepstakes tickets. But I decided to buy a few lottery tickets myself, now that it was legal. I knew it was gambling and I never felt easy about it. I never gambled before. Well, I took a few chances for charity. I would buy four tickets a week and figured it was for a good cause.

"Then I started thinking about retiring and decided to leave. They gave me a big party and I received the Gallatin Award for High Esteem, Public Service, and Integrity. Even though I had a pension of $10,000, I had to pay $2,000 taxes on it and I was still paying off my husband's medical bills— $14,000. I was desperate, so I took a part-time job as a court clerk, where I logged new cases. It was like jumping from the frying pan into the fire. I worked there for just four days. I didn't like it because it was boring. I quit on Thursday, and on Friday I won $250,000 in the lottery.

"I had a four-leaf clover for twenty years under my blotter, and that morning I was going through my papers and that thing fell right at my feet. I won that money in a supermarket right across the street from where my husband is buried. I went to visit him that morning. It was like an omen.

"At first I was depressed. It didn't hit me. I lost a month's sleep. You develop a fear—what's going to happen to me now? When I was spending this money so freely, I kept thinking, 'Is this mine? I didn't work for it.' "

But now, at fifty-five, Angela has adjusted well. She travels a lot, has bought stylish clothes, redecorated her apartment, purchased a new Ford, and is being romanced by an old friend—her former supervisor at the IRS, a widower who retired the same day she did. They have many common interests, including the office they open a few months each year to assist people in filing their taxes. He is teaching her golf and they are contemplating marriage. "Love," he said to me philosophically, "is far more important than wealth. If she didn't have a dime, I'd love her just as much."

We have seen that many widows were confused and shocked. They were fearful of other people, and often unsure of themselves. With their husbands' passing came a period of readjustment which left them lonely and sometimes isolated. Yet, if winning precipitated new crises, it also gave them security and comfort, and materially improved their lives. It was, as Minnie Petraglia put it, "a godsend."

CHAPTER 6

Killing Dreams and Golden Geese: Taxes

"A lottery is properly a tax upon unfortunate self-conceited fools. The world abounds in such fools; it is not fit that every man that will may cheat every man that would be cheated. Rather it is ordained that the Sovereign should have guard of these fools, even as in the case of lunatics and idiots."

—SIR WILLIAM PETTY,
seventeenth-century English economist

Of all the bitter pills lottery winners had to take, taxes were the hardest to swallow. More hard feelings, misunderstandings, and resentment were generated by tax obligations than by any other source of irritation. Taxes on winnings were perceived as a form of harassment, unfair and even un-American. Numerous complaints were expressed about rude representatives of the Internal Revenue Service, harassing audits, and outright belligerence from agents of federal, state, and local taxing authorities. Some resentment no doubt resulted from winners' misunderstandings of tax laws and the extent of their obligations. Many people underestimated the effect the winnings would have on their taxes, and their bewilderment was complicated by the torrent of unsolicited advice from family, friends, and strangers.

Most people felt their winnings should have been tax-free. Many, especially lump-sum winners, had to surrender more than half their prizes. A few had to pay income taxes to three levels of government: city, state, and federal. Several people quit working because they reasoned it was pointless to continue since their winnings put them into a tax bracket which consumed most of their wages. Some winners, like Eunice Baylor, were in dire economic straits and could have used the full amount.

At fifty-five, Eunice was widowed, unemployed, and suffering from a cardiac condition. She was living with one of her three daughters in a rural western New York area, receiving free room and board, but her dependence was demoralizing. She wanted to be free to live where she chose, not indebted to anyone.

"I wanted to work at something—to help out a little. I was unemployed for five years and had hardly any income, just a little from some baby-sitting I was doing. I tried to get jobs, but couldn't. I got a little in the way of insurance when my husband died fifteen years ago, but that was all gone. I went for one interview after another, but they didn't want to hire old ladies with heart conditions. I was living with Mary, my daughter, and it really started to bother me. I felt bad. You just don't want to stay with someone and not give them anything. So I finally got up the courage and I called the welfare people to find out if I could get something to pay my daughter for room and board, and they said I could. I made an appointment to see them the following week, and then I won the $100,000 and never went in. But if I had taken any money, I would have paid them right back."

She will never forget the events of the day she won.

"I was suffering from high blood pressure at the time. One of my other daughters called me and cried over the phone. She didn't say anything at first, she just cried. I thought something was wrong and then she told me that I won. I got scared and passed out. A little boy I was baby-sitting was with me at the time; he couldn't speak, but began to cry. A girl upstairs heard him and came down and she found me on the floor. My daughter heard the phone drop and came up from her home forty-five miles away. I was in a state of shock and couldn't stand up for several hours. My legs were numb. Then I had a crying spell."

Eunice had never had an easy life and looked forward to a more affluent life-style.

"My husband and father were laborers. I had fourteen brothers and sisters and I never had much after my husband died. I just figured things would stay the same unless I remarried. Now I could do the things I always wanted—travel, buy a mink stole and a Persian lamb coat. But then I found out about the taxes. This lottery—they say you win $100,000 and then take it all away in taxes. They took $61,000 from me. I even had a lawyer help, but there wasn't much he could do. He went through everything and couldn't find a way to save me money. I always put at least four names on the ticket except this time. When I went down to get my money, there were men from the IRS waiting there. They told me how much I had to pay and that I must pay immediately. When I complained that the taxes were too much, one of them said, 'If you don't want to pay taxes, you can go to a foreign country, lady. But don't ever come back to the U.S. or we'll get you.' I said it was unfair, and he said, 'Lady, aren't you satisfied with $39,000? For a dollar, what do you want, lady?' The taxes were the only thing that hurt."

Her spirits were dampened, but Eunice decided to make the best of it. She traveled to England and Spain, bought the furs she had always wanted, and rented her own apartment. That was seven years ago, and now the money is gone. At sixty-two, she has no assets except her fur coats and some secondhand furniture. She rents a three-room apartment for $50 a month in a decaying section of downtown Buffalo, not far from the black ghetto. The apartment is within walking distance of the market where she works part-time as a checker for $2 an hour. She takes home $24 a week from her job and receives $146 a month from Social Security, and she

buys lottery tickets religiously, two a week, hoping that light-
ning will strike twice.

Cases such as this were not isolated. In Buffalo I found
Mildred O'Brien and her daughter Judith living on the brink
of poverty, though they had won $100,000 five years before.
Mildred is seventy and Judith forty. They are unemployed
and live in an old two-story house. Mildred's husband, an iron
worker, was killed in an industrial accident in 1945. She gets
no pension. After taxes Mildred and Judith each netted about
$24,000.

Judith recalled, "I spoke with three tax lawyers and they
couldn't do anything for us. We were both on Social Security,
too."

Mildred has a strong desire to work, but is hampered by a
lack of marketable skills and her age. In the past, she worked
occasionally as a domestic for as little as $5 a day, but this
work is now too arduous for her. Judith, too, would like to
work, but cannot because she suffers from rheumatoid arthritis. She has been hospitalized at least once in each of the last
six years. Eighteen months ago she had a plastic joint inserted
in her hip, but the operation had limited success. During our
conversation she periodically rose and walked around the
room because it was painful for her to sit. She takes large
doses of painkillers, and last year her drug bill was over
$2,000.

"I owe the pharmacist $500 now. We ran out of money last
year. It all went so fast. I had medical bills. I paid $1,200 to
one hospital and $600 in doctor's bills. Then I bought $500
worth of clothes, but not all at once. I really didn't do anything extravagant. I bought them over six months. My
mother bought this house with $20,000 of her winnings, and
I spent $6,500 for siding on it. I gave my brother $2,000. He's
a teacher with six kids.

"Right now I wish I was able to work. Up until a year ago
I worked as a hat-check girl in a local restaurant. I could
make $75 to $100 on a Saturday night, but I've been too ill
to work. Before that I was a secretary for six years. I used to

think it was boring, but now that I'm not working, it seems interesting.

"I don't like having to depend on people for too much. I have a friend who comes here to do the cleaning once a week because I'm not able. She's very nice, but some things you like to do your own way and yet I don't feel that I can stand there and give her orders.

"Right now I have over $7,000 in medical bills. Blue Cross wouldn't pay my bill a couple of years ago. They said it was a pre-existing illness. Last year I went in the hospital for the same reason and they paid it. I don't know how we manage. We get about $4,000 from various sources—Social Security, rent from the tenant upstairs. I'm trying to get on Medicaid. I can imagine what it's like on welfare. A woman at Medicaid called me a thief. I showed her my drug bills and she said it couldn't possibly be that much.

"Life is just existing. There's nothing to do and nowhere to go from here. I look forward to nights so another day goes by. What is it that Norman Vincent Peale says?—'Thank God, another day.' I say, 'God, oh, God, another day.'"

In addition to being poor and unemployed, the O'Briens and Eunice Baylor had something else in common: they won in 1968, the year Congress imposed a ten-percent income-tax surcharge. This temporary levy would ordinarily have meant little to people in their low income brackets, but, as luck would have it, an extra chunk was skimmed off the top of their $100,000 prizes.

Dr. Martin Friedmann, a radiologist in the Buffalo area, and one of the few winners already in the upper income bracket, also won $100,000 that year.

"I bought three tickets at the bank and put them in my wife's name. I thought she was lucky. She didn't even know about it. They were the first tickets I ever bought. When I bought them, I thought, 'Yes, I'm gonna win!' I don't know why, but I had this strange feeling.

"There was some resentment about it around here. People talked about it—'Oh, he's a doctor. Why did *he* win?' But it's a funny thing. I had been on the staff of a hospital until that year. I was being paid a nice salary, but nothing compared to what I could have made in private practice. The year I won I went into private practice. It had nothing to do with winning, it just happened that way. It doubled my income and I was left with only $30,000 of the winnings after taxes. I wanted to put it into the kids' names to cut down on the taxes, but they wouldn't let me. Now you can. If I won again, I'd give the money to the children, definitely."

Some people were not as sanguine about paying their taxes. Many distraught and disillusioned winners had shouting matches with IRS representatives after learning of their tax liabilities. Even small winners had to relinquish large chunks of their windfalls. The average tax on a $50,000 lump-sum win was $23,000. This ranged from a low of $15,000 for a priest whose earnings were $2,200 to a high of $28,000 for a family with a regular income of $20,000. Bill Lawrence, a sixty-year-old metallurgist, held the dubious distinction of paying the highest taxes on his $50,000 win:

"I fought the IRS for four years over how much they could take. I was right, too. Even so, I finally paid them all they wanted. We live in a police state now!"

Among the millionaires who receive their winnings in twenty annual $50,000 installments, first-year federal income taxes ranged from $9,000 to $24,000.* Average first-year taxes were $17,000, but figures varied greatly because of differences in earnings, marital status, number of dependents and exemptions, and IRS discretionary rulings. Here are a few examples of variations in taxes. Two widows, one forty-one with four dependents, the other fifty-nine with no dependents, earned approximately $7,000 before they each won a million dollars. The first paid $12,000 in federal income taxes and the second paid $18,000, while a forty-year-old father of three with comparable earnings paid $9,200. A thirty-three-year-old railroad worker, the father of three,

*Federal law now requires that 20 percent be withheld from winnings over $5,000, so million-dollar winners receive annual checks of $40,000.

and his wife had a combined income of $23,000 and paid $12,000 in federal income taxes on their first installment, while a sixty-three-year-old bartender earned $7,000 and paid $15,000. A fifty-one-year-old plumber and his wife had a combined income of $16,000 and paid $11,000, but a thirty-nine-year-old service-station manager with three dependent children earned $11,000 and paid $19,000 in taxes.

Taxes on early installments are lower than later ones because most winners income-average their returns. After five years this tactic is generally ineffective, and unless shelters or loopholes are found, winners may have to return as much as half of their prizes in taxes. One winner accepted this stoically: "I don't think this is right, but I refuse to use loopholes. Only Nixon could pay $900 in taxes."

Some variation was attributable to the uneven quality of the advice winners received. Two millionaire winners tried figuring taxes on their own and have fared well. Two others utilized mass-production tax-return firms and paid what most people in their income levels did. The rest of the millionaires obtained more specialized advice from lawyers, accountants, and banks. Some also sought aid from State Lottery Commissions and the Internal Revenue Service. But even professional opinions can have unwanted ramifications.

Anthony Giambrone, a thirty-four-year-old bachelor, won his million on Friday the thirteenth, six months before we spoke, but he did not completely escape the jinx. Tony lives with his sixty-seven-year-old mother in an old single-family house in the southern part of New Jersey. The region is flat, sandy, and desolate, dotted with scruffy pines, inhabited by few people. I found him leaning over a Rototiller between two rows of grapevines in the backyard, and he began detailing his financial problems.

"I was working as a dental technician for nine years. A dentist friend of mine got me into it. He put me to work for him in his lab, where I learned to make dentures and work with gold. I really liked it and I was making $185 a week, but right after I won I got laid off. They had two younger guys there who hadn't been there as long, but they kept them. I guess they needed the money more than me, but I want to work. Once in a while they call me in and I work a day or a day and a half for them. If they need me, I go. I've been to three or four places trying to get back to work. I'll take anything.

"People say to me, 'Why work? You don't have to. You've got this money coming in.' The guys at work would say that. So I bought them a couple of tickets and said, 'Here, have a blast!'

"And on top of everything, I don't have any money. I haven't touched that money I won. I haven't enjoyed it. My lawyer and the bank invested it for me. They put it all in some kind of government bonds where I can't touch it. I didn't expect to get laid off. I'm supposed to get the money in May, but in the meantime I have to pay for lots of different insurances and that cleaned me out. I've had to use all my own savings. I even had to use my own money to make a trip to California to see my grandmother. So far, everybody's enjoyed the money—the lawyers, the bank—everybody except me. The only thing I ever bought with it was a suit and a sport jacket for my trip. I thought I'd have money coming in. I never thought I'd get laid off. I never had a problem like this. I'm broke now, but I wouldn't even think of collecting unemployment. There are so many poor people. Could you see me there?

"Let me tell you, all the advice I got was clear as mud. I'm gonna change that next year. They told me I'd get money when I needed it for taxes. So far, I spent $2,000 of my own for the first two tax payments. I'm gonna have to make a big tax payment in a month. It'll be around $15,000 and I don't know what I'm gonna do.

"Just staying around here doing nothing, you get awful nervous. I even started turning gray. [He pointed to a spot on his head.] I'd stay up till four or five in the morning worrying and thinking about it. I never had anything to worry about before."

Some winners, like Eunice Baylor and Bill Lawrence, felt that no amount of advice could help. It seemed that the IRS was waging a personal vendetta against them. Although many avaricious hucksters eye big winners greedily, few are as successful as the IRS in extracting money from them. Several people reported experiences like that of cab driver Peter Pulaski, a $100,000 winner.

"After I won, I was interviewed on TV. They asked me a lot of questions about what I was going to do with the money and then I told them I had $67,000 after taxes. Do you know that the next day two men from the IRS went to my accountant's office. They said that I hadn't paid enough in taxes. But that wasn't true. As soon as I won, I got an accountant and we went over the whole thing. I told him I didn't care how much it cost—to do it the right way. He was very upset that they came over—it didn't look good for him. They stayed there for two days and made me pay another $400. I was really burned."

A similar experience befell Mrs. Walter Johnson, the wife of a New Jersey millionaire winner. The Johnsons gave their daughters large sums of money for down payments on houses. One day Mrs. Johnson received a phone call from a man purporting to be a researcher. "He wanted to know if he could ask me a few questions about the lottery and what we were doing with the money. He told me that everything would be confidential. We got to talking about different things, and I guess I mentioned the money we gave to our daughters. The next day I was reading the local paper and there it was. Everything I had said! He was really a reporter."

"Well," Walter interjected, "apparently the income-tax people saw it and they called me in for an audit. They said I couldn't give that much away without it being taxed. They took another $700 from me, and I'm sure they're gonna audit me every year now."

Such confrontations do not endear the local tax offices to winners. But one shrewd woman, who has won several thousand dollars on different occasions, firmly believes her compliant demeanor affects the tax outcome.

"You can't yell at them and you can't gyp them. I go right down to the IRS for help in finding out how much I owe. I can get a whole staff of lawyers if I want. I was in business for thirty-two years and I learned a lot, but I just go down there dumb as a bunny and let them figure it out."

A few others realized they might have a considerable tax obligation and went directly to the IRS for help. Some received valuable assistance, and others, like Charles Dornhoffer, were the butt of jokes:

"As soon as I won, I thought about the taxes. The next day I wrote to the IRS and explained that I had just won a million dollars in the New Jersey lottery and could they give me any information on my tax responsibilities. I didn't know anything. I thought I might even have to pay the following week. You know what they did? They sent me back my own letter and wrote across it, 'Congratulations to you and to us,' and they stuck an IRS address label on it. That's the kind of professionalism and help they gave me."

Taxes have figured prominently in the Dornhoffers' lives since then. Charlie had planned to retire when he was sixty and had accumulated $150,000 in company stock. Now his carefully laid plans were shattered by his unexpected good fortune. He petitioned for early retirement, but his company waffled.

"Of course, I could have left, but my stock would have been taxed heavily, as income rather than as a long-term gain, if I waited until the normal retirement age. I decided to wait for the company's decision and work for another year and a half. Then the company announced it was changing its policy and set fifty-seven as the age for retirement. I think this was because of me. Anyway, it was a funny coincidence."

As soon as the policy change was implemented, Charlie and his wife retired. Although he retained a tax lawyer and an accountant, he was not able to avoid paying $40,000 in taxes two years ago when he disposed of half his stock. Beside his annual $50,000 lottery check, he receives $200 a month from his former employer. He calculates he nets $44 out of this.

The old cliché that nothing is certain except death and taxes could become the swan song of state lotteries if antiquated tax laws are not modernized to accommodate winners' sudden windfalls. Many lottery experts, including the National Commission on Gambling, believe taxes on winnings affect ticket sales adversely. Most countries don't tax winnings. For example, million-dollar winners in the Canadian lotteries are given the money in a lump sum *tax-free*. But in the United States even dying does not let winners off the tax hook. While winners and ticket-buyers are indignant over high income taxes, inheritance taxes are more onerous because the estate of a deceased winner is taxed heavily and promptly. Yet many winners do not know their winnings are part of their estate even though they have not received all the installments.

Federal and state inheritance taxes must be paid within a specified time, or substantial interest penalties are levied against the unpaid balance. In many states, inheritance taxes are assessed according to the relationship of the beneficiaries to the deceased. In New Jersey, for example, the tax schedule carries a $5,000 exemption each for the decedent's father, mother, grandparents, husband or wife, and children, who are considered Class A beneficiaries,* but no exemption is given for a brother, sister, wife or widow of a son of a decedent husband or widower of a daughter, or any other beneficiaries named (termed Class C beneficiaries) if the sum is in excess of $500. Inheritance taxes can wreak havoc among unsuspecting heirs of big lottery winners who are responsible for paying taxes on money they will not receive for many years.

To dramatize the impact of these taxes, let us assume that John Smith won a million dollars on January 1, 1975, in the New Jersey lottery. On that day he received a check for

*For beneficiaries of people dying on or after July 1, 1978, the exemption increases to $15,000.

$49,500 from the state (he had already received a $500 check for being in the finals). Disasters sometimes happen, and for the sake of discussion we must kill Mr. Smith in a car accident that night on his way home from a party celebrating his good luck. John's only heir is his wife. Under New Jersey inheritance-tax law, she receives a $5,000 exemption, but must pay $34,800 in state inheritance taxes on $550,000, which is the approximate dollar value of the unpaid installments.* The $550,000 figure is the current value of the winnings, which are actually an annuity the state has purchased from an insurance company in the winner's name. It varies depending on the age of the winner. The state pays the first $50,000 installment and then purchases an annuity in the winner's name from an insurance company, which agrees to pay the remaining nineteen. The state uses the money from the sale of tickets for whatever purpose is designated by law. The insurance company benefits because it invests the money and earns a higher rate than it pays out.

Let us return to Mrs. Smith, because there are complications. New Jersey law stipulates that the inheritance tax must be paid within eight months of the decedent's death, or a ten-percent interest penalty will be charged on the unpaid portion. Nor is this the end of her financial obligations, for there is a federal counterpart to the state tax. Even with a substantial marital deduction, she must pay approximately $41,000 in federal taxes within nine months or a nine-percent interest penalty is annually levied against the estate.

This hypothetical example was designed to show what could happen in case of a winner's death. As fate would have it, this has already happened.

Evelyn Bollis was a seventy-nine-year-old widow who lived for many years in a quiet residential area outside Newark, New Jersey. Although the homes were old, they were kept in good condition. The neighborhood was particularly appealing to her because three relatives lived on the same block.

*These figures were computed without considering exemptions or deductions granted under state tax law.

About a year and a half ago Evelyn's health began to fail. She developed a stomach ailment which required surgery, and the medical bills began mounting. In an effort to economize, she sold her home and moved to an inexpensive apartment in a nearby city. Her condition worsened, and she required a nurse-companion, Ruby Brown. Ruby would buy lottery tickets for her at a local supermarket, and one day they were surprised to learn she was in the finals. Too ill to go herself, Evelyn asked Ruby to stand in for her at the drawing. The rest is history: she won the million.

"I used to buy her two tickets every week," said Ruby, "and she never even had a number right. She was about ready to quit, and then she said she'd try the Clover Club [a plan whereby a player subscribes to the same number] for six months. I remember saying, 'When you win, you're going to hit the whole thing,' and she did."

A year and a half later Evelyn's condition deteriorated and she died. Although she didn't have a chance to enjoy the money in the usual way—no new cars, homes, or luxury items were bought, no trips taken—the money did comfort her.

"She was able to afford the best care," recalled Ruby. "She had special-duty nurses round the clock. She was in the finest hospital with a private room. If she hadn't won the money, she wouldn't have been able to have the kind of care she had. It kept her alive."

Evelyn had no children and left only distant relatives (Class C beneficiaries). When she won, she made a will to provide for the distribution of the installments. Realizing that large inheritance taxes would have to be paid upon her death, her attorneys included a provision to sell the unpaid balance of the installments for a lump sum at a discount. In this way, a large sum of money could be raised to pay inheritance taxes and the remainder could be distributed to the beneficiaries. However, New Jersey law forbids this, and consequently her estate cannot be settled for twenty years. In addition to inheritance taxes, federal income taxes must be paid each year on the new installment, and lawyers' fees must be deducted from the estate to pay for their services.

I spoke with the lawyer who is handling the Bollis estate.

"She was aware of the problem before she died. She even cut out a few newspaper clippings about the tax problem and sent them to me. I incorporated the clause about selling the installments in case the law might be changed at some time in the future. I thought it might be possible to sell to an insurance company, providing we didn't take a bath.

"When it became obvious that no change was forthcoming, I met with the lottery commission. I showed them how the estate was being penalized for nonpayment of taxes by one branch of the state government because they were withholding the money. I must say they were unmoved. They took a traditional bureaucratic approach to the whole thing. They said they didn't care what another branch of the government did. Later I was able to show the tax people that there was insufficient liquidity in the estate and hence a reasonable cause for not paying the taxes on time. They reduced the interest penalty to six percent, but, with all of the interest and penalties and taxes, it will be three to four years before a dime of lottery winnings becomes available. We have to soak up the tax burdens first. The unfortunate thing is that many of her heirs are old and can use the money now, but they may not live to collect any."

There are few things winners can do to ease the inheritance-tax burden. Some take out life-insurance policies in the sum of the estimated taxes. Annual premiums vary depending on one's marital status and age, but they are high—frequently in excess of $2,000, and some people pay over $5,000. One alert million-dollar winner, an insurance salesman, immediately took out a policy to cover the possibility of such a catastrophe. We discussed the problem.

"Why, you *have* to take out an insurance policy to cover you. What you do is get an estimate on the amount your relatives would have to pay in taxes if you died and take out a life-insurance policy for it. It's a form of savings anyway—

maybe not the best, but it's all right. It averages about $2,100 a year for a person at age forty, but that's not much compared to the tax you'd have to pay. For a single person around forty who won a million and died, the average inheritance tax would be around $230,000. For a married person that age, it would be around $150,000. Payable in nine months! Both husband and wife should have policies, because if they both died, then their children would have to pay the taxes. It sounds screwy and unfair, but that's the law.

"Most lawyers don't even know it. People go to them and think they are specialists on every kind of legal matter, but that's impossible. I used to think they knew everything, too. Then, after I studied insurance, I would be at a party or someplace with them and hear them talk, and they just didn't know anything about this kind of stuff. But they wouldn't admit it to anyone.

"You know, even my own wife wouldn't believe me. Even though it's my business. She just didn't think they could tax us that much."

She interrupted: "That's true. I didn't think they could. I just didn't go along with him. Then one day I was watching the *Dinah Shore Show* and someone was on, I think it was Shelly Fabray. She was talking about all the trouble she was having with inheritance taxes, and I called my husband in. He was outside in the garden and I was yelling to him, 'Come in and see this. You were right!'

"But even to this day she hasn't bought a policy for herself. She still doesn't realize that if we both died, our sons would have to pay the taxes."

She smiled, looked a little uneasy, and admitted she probably should take out a policy, yet the next moment exclaimed, "But there really doesn't seem to be a need for it."

"It wasn't any different with the other winners," her husband continued. "I spoke with all of the first winners. I tried to convince them of the importance of getting themselves insured. Some of them understood. Six of them bought policies. One of the guys doesn't quite understand the whole thing, but we are friendly and he respects my judgment about this. The rest resisted. They thought I was just trying to sell them insurance policies for my own gain. I tried to explain it to them, but, you know, there are all kinds of people, and some were very suspicious after they won. All I can say is that I tried. I told every winner. I have a clear conscience."

Inheritance taxes are a very real problem for *any* winner whose prize is paid in installments, yet many are unaware of this. Even the few winners who were familiar with the full ramifications of the law had a cavalier attitude, despite the fact that thirteen of the fifty-four millionaires were sixty or older, and several were in failing health. The full impact of inheritance taxes was, in essence, overlooked, ignored, and misunderstood. Obviously, there is a void here that the state could fill by providing advice and reforming antiquated inheritance-tax laws which can turn heirs of instant millionaires into instant paupers. Federal and state governments might begin by deferring payments on deceased winners' estates and waiving penalties until there is sufficient liquidity to pay the tax.

To escape from the clutches of government, which they know would get a large share of the money if the winner died before receiving all the installments, three families intentionally spend all their winnings. Many others give large amounts to children and relatives and eschew investing because of their advanced age—"There's no need for that now" —or the low return they would receive because of income taxes.

As Charlie Dornhoffer put it, "I try to spend it every year. I made no investments. You give a lot away. I put a new roof on my father-in-law's house, fixed up the inside. I also bought a house for one of my daughters, and we have given the other one $18,000 so far. I bought a Cadillac and some jewelry for my wife and put some money into this house. I won $25 twice in the lottery since then. I gave it to my father-in-law. He could use it and they would have taxed me."

Even winners of lesser amounts chose to spend the money rather than invest it because they didn't want to give the government any more in taxes.

Bill Lawrence was so piqued that he and his wife consumed the money immediately. "It's all spent. I spent it in part to get out of paying taxes and get even with the IRS. I put it in the bank just long enough to write checks on it. We took a longer vacation than usual. We had been getting a new car every year—a Chevy Caprice. Now we jumped to a Riviera. We gave most of the rest away; $14,000 went to our kids. We paid off our old car and gave it to one of them, and we bought a new one for the other one. We gave the money away to all kinds of people. Some who needed it (so they said), but they never repaid it. I gave $250 to the superintendent of my apartment building and he took off. We never saw him again."

A few shrewd investors bought property so they could receive tax breaks, but most people did not know about, or were too conservative to utilize, this legitimate shelter. (We will explore the nature of their investments in the next chapter.)

Considerable animosity was engendered toward all levels of government over the taxation issue. This hostility left most winners bitter and politically alienated. They felt jilted by the lottery and the government, but helpless about righting what they considered a grave injustice.

It sometimes seems as if government will go to any length to get the little man. An illustration of this came to light in January 1971 when Pascual Martinez, a fifty-four-year-old unemployed tobacco worker from Puerto Rico, won $100,-000 in the New York State Lottery. Like thousands of his countrymen, Martinez came to the mainland to seek a better life for himself and his family. But his wife died shortly after they settled in Connecticut, leaving him to care for four young children, one of whom was crippled. He had to quit work and was receiving $100 a week from the Welfare Department for subsistence. Then one day in December 1970 he bought a lottery ticket on a trip to New York City. In Connecticut, welfare payments are regarded as loans that must be repaid whenever possible, and when the Connecticut Department of Welfare learned of Martinez's good fortune, it prevailed on Albany to withhold $25,000 of his winnings, which it claimed he owed the state for the welfare payments he had received during the past five years. The federal tax on the remainder was estimated to be $46,000, and he was also removed from the welfare rolls (*The New York Times,* January 14, 1971, p. 39).

In April 1972, Henry C. White, Welfare Commissioner of Connecticut, showed how technology and individual initiative can be used to recoup even small amounts of lost revenue for the state. He had the names of Connecticut lottery winners run through the Welfare Department's computer to match recipients with winners. This procedure turned up seven $400 winners among welfare recipients, and they were forced to give their prizes to the Welfare Department. People who had already spent their winnings would not escape because, White averred, the money would be deducted from their future checks (*The New York Times,* April 19, 1972, p. 30).

In August 1974, Nicholas Zabol, a fifty-five-year-old unemployed civil engineer born in the Soviet Union who became a United States citizen in 1966, received a bill for $7,422 from the New York City Human Resources Administration after he won $10,000 in the New York State Lottery. Under New York Social Services Law, people who inherit or acquire money through prizes are required to repay what they have received. Zabol had been receiving aid since August 1970. He had hoped to enroll in a twenty-two-month computer-programming course at New York University and use the money "to get off welfare, learn a new profession, and go back to work." But now he declared despondently, "Winning is too much losing" (*The New York Times*, August 23, 1974, p. 33).

Such stories do little to allay winners' suspicions that state and federal bureaucrats discriminate against average citizens and favor entrenched wealth. Indeed, recent publications of the Internal Revenue Service reveal that in 1974, 672 nontaxable returns were filed reporting adjusted gross incomes between $50,000 and $1 million and five nontaxable returns showed adjusted gross incomes of $1 million or more.

Despite the pronouncements of lottery officials about their opposition to taxation of winnings, there has been little movement to change the laws. The final report of the National Commission on Gambling did, however, recommend that winnings be tax-exempt. If the track record of recent recommendations of national commissions on such topics as population, drugs, and pornography is indicative, immediate action will not be forthcoming, but reforms may well occur as lotteries spread to other states. If lottery officials are in earnest about the taxation issue, they might persuade their legislatures to exempt winners from state income and inheritance taxes, setting an example for the federal government,* which might be enticed to exempt a percentage of lottery revenues from taxes.

Of course, the opposite position about taxation is also persuasive. Proponents of taxing contend that winners should not be exempted and should share the burden like everyone else. In a recent conversation, Henry Luther III, former director of the New Jersey State Lottery, stanchly defended the taxing of winners:

"The other lottery directors can't believe me. But look, if you are going to tax the poor guy who makes his living by digging a ditch, then why not tax these people? They didn't even work to get their money. After all, it's only fair. I don't think it's a real issue."

Nevertheless, the public is being sold the promise of instant wealth, and taxes make this promise hollow. Winners are subjected to quadruple taxation. They pay income taxes on the money they earn to buy tickets. The state withholds

*New Jersey's recently enacted income tax exempts prizes of lottery winners.

a percentage of the money from ticket purchases for operating expenses. Their winnings are taxed as income (sometimes by three levels of government). Finally, their estates are taxed after their death. In the lottery, the biggest winners are the state and federal governments, because they get you coming and going.

CHAPTER 7

Where the Money Goes: Spending, Saving, and Squandering

"Money is like muck, not good except it be spread."
—FRANCIS BACON, *Of Seditions and Troubles*

There is a very special club in New Jersey with a small, highly select membership. The odds that you will be able to join are twenty million to one—if you buy New Jersey lottery tickets. The club is the Millionaire's Club and the members have each won a million dollars in the lottery. The club was started in 1971 as a publicity gimmick. Initially, four meetings a year were held around the state. Members wanting to attend functions paid annual dues of $200 which covered the cost of dinners. There was more dining and dancing at meetings than business, but as the membership grew, sentiment arose for inviting guests to speak about investments, taxes, and insurance. Some winners, however, were antagonistic toward this idea. Most had already received a surfeit of advice and were skeptical and suspicious of strangers' motives, and so the practice was abandoned. A suggestion that members establish an investment corporation met opposition. One proponent of the plan lamented, "We could each put up $1,000 a year and we'd have a sizable amount of capital after a while, but there were too many different people, and they all had their own ideas about what they should do. They could never get together."

The divergence of opinion also meant there was little that members had in common, and gradually attendance at club meetings declined. As one member put it, "I don't need to pay $200 to go out to dinner. I can do that right here for less." Most recent winners do not know much about the club even though they are members. Their only contact with other winners may have occurred during a brief exchange of congratulations at their drawing. Some early club members have become good friends and regularly entertain each other in their new homes. This nucleus meets once or twice a year, but efforts to rejuvenate the club have not been successful.

The demise of an active club is regrettable, for winners, especially new ones, need counseling and guidance. The support and information they could obtain from the club might help them cope with the problems they experience and the life changes they undergo. The transition from poor to affluent, from struggling to secure, is difficult for people who are thrust from obscurity into the limelight. Robert Whelan, the forty-three-year-old president of the club and New Jersey's first million-dollar winner, is convinced from his own experience that the group could be extremely beneficial. The novelty of Whelan's big win made him an instant celebrity. He was the subject of numerous newspaper stories and appeared on four television shows, including Mike Douglas's, and a number of radio programs. The New York *Daily News* broke his story in large headlines. This is his favorite clipping. ("We wiped [Lt.] Calley right off the front page.") Four years later he is still asked for interviews. Friends around the country send clippings about him from their local papers. One sent a postcard recently wishing him luck, but advised, "Bolt the doors and lock the windows."

Lately, Bob has been having second thoughts about the publicity. "Every time you do an article, you're not sure what kind of kooks are out there and what they might do." He has also become wary of reporters after he was "burned" by one from the now defunct Newark *Evening News*. "Some of the things she said about us were not true. She just made them up."

He thought he would receive a lot of mail after winning, but the amount and duration exceeded his expectations. "We got loads of mail. It lasted for more than two years. There were letters from all kinds of people. They asked me questions, wished me luck, and offered me all kinds of propositions. People wanted me to invest in insurance, stocks, and all sorts of schemes. One of the most intriguing offers came from a man who had a patent on a new engine. He claimed it was better than the Wankel, but I didn't send him any money."

The day I spoke with Bob, his wife gave birth to their fifth child. "We had two before I won, and she was pregnant with the third at the time. Three probably would have been tops. Especially today with the cost of raising a family. But I love kids. My mother comes from a family of twenty-one."

The Whelans live in a beautiful two-story home in an expensive suburban area in northern New Jersey. "We were looking at this house even before we won, but it would have been tight." After winning they sold their old home and moved in. However, they have limited their expenses in other areas. Bob takes pride in being cost-conscious and budgeting. They bought a Ford station wagon, selected on the basis of utility, not frills. "I like Ford products. I always thought it would be nice to get a Continental Mark IV, but I didn't get one and I can afford it."

Bob confessed that in the beginning he lacked confidence in his ability to make financial decisions. "I was really worried about handling the money. I went to every investment-counseling meeting in town. I'd spend two or three nights a week. I learned a lot. Now I know more than many stockbrokers do. I was even going to take a test to be a dealer in mutual funds."

Bob relies heavily on judicious bookkeeping to get the most out of his annual $50,000 check. "I budget everything.

As soon as the check comes, I put $20,000 dollars in one bank for taxes. They run $22,000. I put $15,000 in tax-free municipal bonds, and a little in the market—just a little. Ten percent of my salary from work goes into a savings plan. I take the dividends from the bonds and save it up. When I get $5,000, I reinvest it in more bonds.

"It's difficult to hold down buying urges. Budgeting is a real problem. You have fantasies, but you realize that the money isn't as much as you anticipated. I'm very conservative. If it's too much, I do without it. Like $3 for a pound of sugar. I tell my wife to leave it alone." To demonstrate his lack of interest in materialistic commodities, he mentioned offhandedly, "I don't even have a color TV. Mine broke six months ago and I haven't had it fixed yet."

The Whelans have made some concessions to suburban living. They joined a country club (principally because Bob likes to play golf), and he admits he plays more now than before he won. Membership dues are $1,000 a year, and they had to purchase a $2,000 bond in the club to join (after being carefully screened). It was in the area of social relationships that Bob feared he would encounter his greatest difficulties. He works as a supervisor in a utility company and was not sure he would be accepted into this professional community.

"I've never been that outgoing, but I'm associating with different people now. I always had some problems at functions—I'm a little uneasy at times. We're traveling in different circles now, but when you come right down to it, all people are pretty much the same. There's good and bad in any class system."

Now he realizes his fears were unfounded. His neighbors are friendly, and he and his wife have made many new friends, "not because I won, but because I moved and met new people." Of course, there are those who try to ingratiate themselves because of his winnings, "but you can spot them right away. Within half an hour they're asking for money."

Because Bob was the target of hucksters, he appreciated the need for specialized counseling and encouraged winners to participate in the club and listen to speakers.

"Some of these fellows were very sharp. They weren't trying to sell anything. They were there as a favor to me, but they weren't always treated very well. Some of the people thought they were just trying to push their own interests. At first, some were attentive, but interest in them began to disappear. A few of the more rowdy ones gave them a hard time at meetings and kept interrupting them. People just couldn't appreciate what they were trying to do for them. I really learned a lot, and I wish they would have listened. But you know how suspicious they are."

When the experiment failed, the winners were left to their own devices. Bob was one of the few who made a conscientious effort to learn about investment opportunities. A few fortunate others, like Charles Dornhoffer (who, as we saw in the last chapter, intentionally spends his annual installments), were financially secure before they won.

The Dornhoffers lived in a comfortable house in a northern New Jersey city. Charlie had a secure job as a soap salesman with a national manufacturing company, and his wife worked as a clerk in a nearby school. Their two daughters were married.

"I finally saw the light at the end of the tunnel. I made my last payment on my younger daughter's tuition for college. Then I told my wife, 'Let's get a car for your birthday.' The one we had was ten years old. I thought our lives would get better. Both kids were married and had an education. It was clear sailing. Then they called me up on the stage. That was icing on the cake.

"I knew I was going to win. Our number was the last prize drawn of the twenty they gave away that day. When they called me, up I went onstage with my hands clasped over my head. I looked pretty calm. The governor was there. He had just come from Washington to get permission to have lottery results televised. He looked at me and said, 'You have to be the calmest winner yet.' After all those years of blood, sweat, and tears it was an anticlimax. I even worked that day. When

I left, I told my boss, 'I have to go and win my million dollars in the lottery.' "

Tom and Marge Thompson were also secure before they won. Though not affluent, they were living well on the $20,000 salary that Tom earned as an electronics technician for the government, and they had a comfortable house in a resort town by the ocean. Their two children were in high school, and Marge was preparing to embark on a new career at forty-six. Then they won a million dollars. They sold their house and bought a beautiful $100,000 ranch house in a more exclusive section of town. It rests on an acre of land, and a scenic river borders their backyard.

The money enabled them to move up a notch in socio-economic status, and much of it has been used to extend their recreational activities.

"I get four weeks vacation a year and I used to take it a day at a time," said Tom. "Now I take regular chunks of time for vacations. I exceeded my days already this year. We take one trip a year with the kids and one trip without them. We've been to the Virgin Islands, Jamaica, Florida, Bermuda, and on a cruise. For three straight years before I won we went on vacation and they called me back. They wouldn't think of doing that now. They couldn't find me."

They also purchased a twenty-eight-foot boat for deep-sea fishing, but they found they were using it infrequently. "We took it out only three times last summer," said Tom, "so we sold it and got a small outboard and a sailboat."

Their financial picture was further enhanced when Marge inherited a large sum shortly after they won. Luck seems to run in their family, for two months later Tom's brother hit the lottery for $50,000.

Only five millionaire families, however, were financially well off before winning. Most winners came from humble origins. Being economically and educationally deprived may have narrowed their perspectives on spending and invest-ment, and, while we all like to fantasize about how we would spend a windfall, few winners spent extravagantly. Several items did seem indispensable. First among these "necessities" was an automobile. All but four millionaires bought a new car (two had bought cars shortly before winning), and four bought two new cars. In most cases, winners gravitated toward the traditional status symbols and purchased hefty American sedans. There were five Cadillacs, four Continental Mark IV's, three Oldsmobile 98's, two Oldsmobile Tornadoes, and one Buick Rivera. Despite the high cost of these vehicles, many winners felt their luck had run out when it came to obtaining satisfaction from them. They were particularly upset about the lower mileage than they were accustomed to getting. One disillusioned Cadillac owner remarked: "It's a lemon. It costs me $25 to $30 a week for gas."

Several others had cars which developed serious engine problems. One middle-aged winner drove his new Buick across the country and found it took much longer than expected. "We stopped at every dealer on the way. I kept complaining about the transmission. They said there was nothing wrong—it was my imagination. When I got home, there was a letter for me from the company. They recalled them all for the transmission."

But lifelong ambitions for such cars could not be resisted, even when, as one millionaire found, he could not park his new Fleetwood near his home because the street was too narrow.

Millionaires' largest expenditures were for new homes. Nearly eighty percent moved after winning, and the average cost of the new home was $84,000. Five actually cost over $100,000. Most winners' homes are located in well-heeled bedroom communities—places they had heard of but never expected to reside in. Many feared they would not be accepted by their affluent neighbors, but these anxieties were usually unfounded. Gaining admittance to "higher" social circles could, however, be expensive, as Bob Whelan learned.

The homes were large, averaging nine rooms, decorated in bright colors with flowing floor-length drapes, wall-to-wall carpets, and richly upholstered furniture. Often they were all electric, equipped with the most modern gadgets and conveniences such as intercoms, microwave ovens, and central air-conditioning. Another standard feature was a game room with a pool table, and a monstrous floor-to-ceiling fireplace could usually be found in the living room or den. The houses were often situated on an acre or more of land, and three winners had four or more acres.

The amount of money spent on homes is instructive because in many instances it reveals lack of foresight. New homes were often obviously too large for winners whose children were grown and living elsewhere; or too isolated for people habituated to city life.

The most sobering illustration of imprudence is the monthly mortgage payments, several near $1,000. For a few, the combined cost of mortgage, taxes, utilities, and maintenance runs $1,200 a month. People who had not owned homes previously expended more winnings because they had no equity to put toward the down payment. After income taxes and expenses for the new homes, about a quarter of the winners were left with around $15,000 for the rest of the year. One overextended millionaire admitted: "We're not ashamed to say we made a mistake."

Winners' homes were a tangible symbol of their prizes and security. Much time, energy, and money went into housing, and their efforts were not wasted. The homes are located in highly desirable areas, and their market value is appreciating. Although home-buying exhausted their early installments of winnings, and while they may not be content to live marginally among their wealthy neighbors, the houses made good investments.

Four millionaires who did not move spent $4,500 to $6,000 in remodeling. One family enlarged and redecorated their kitchen; another added a family room; a third family, living in a thirty-five-year-old two-bedroom home, enlarged and redecorated three rooms; and another family built a wall around their house. Three other families had siding put on their homes, and one also had a new roof installed.

Nine families reported furniture expenditures ranging from $3,000 to $10,000. Furnishings were often elaborate; yet several homes looked bare because of their size—another unforeseen contingency accompanying the affluent life-style some winners aspired to. Most people had to reconcile themselves to the fact that they would need several more checks before they could afford to furnish their dream homes.

Two families spent $5,000 for the construction of swimming pools in their backyards, and both regretted it. One complained about maintenance costs; the other had a more fundamental problem: "That pool's a sore subject around here. They put it in last summer. We bought three tankloads of water to fill it. We had the water trucked in because we use well water here and we didn't want to put a strain on our well. It all leaked out in a few days. We wouldn't pay them until they fixed it. All it needs is a new liner. Well, they're suing us and we're suing them, and it sits there empty!"

Other large common expenditures reported by millionaire winners included color TVs, stereo sets, tractor-mowers, washers and dryers, and even a $1,700 piano. Two women purchased expensive jewelry, one of them spending $8,000. Three families spent some of their first checks on clothes, and one woman bought a mink stole. Two other families bought twenty-eight-foot cabin cruisers. One winner purchased a Honda motorcycle for his son, along with numerous other recreational items such as fishing gear, golf clubs, and skiing equipment for his family.

One might expect the list of luxuries and consumer items to be larger, but most winners did not have much money left after buying homes. When they wanted to spend more, they sometimes found themselves being overcharged by local merchants. There were several reports of this, some even involving relatives of winners. One millionaire described his predicament:

"Everything we buy, they see us and double the price. It even happened to my son-in-law. He wanted me to tile his basement and got a price on some tile. I thought it was high, so I checked a few places away from here and found the local price was $200 more than it should have been. They had doubled the price. It's gotten so bad that we have to go out of town to buy big stuff."

Another winner wanted to buy the land adjacent to his mother's house so he could build himself a home, but the price was outlandish. "The guy wants too much. Three years ago he wanted $10,000 for three acres. After I won, I asked him how much and he said $30,000. I never should have asked him. I'm sure he raised the price because of that. The land isn't that good. It's low and swampy.

"That kind of thing has been happening. Since I won, the prices people charge me have gone up. I went to have the tires changed on my car a few weeks ago. All they had to do was take them off and put the other ones on the wheels. They charged me $6 for that. It always cost $3 before. I feel a lot of times I get taken now."

(Incidentally, these two winners live a mile and a half apart.)

Sometimes winners did not look the part of affluent Americans, creating a reverse reaction—skeptical salesmen did not take them seriously. One winner described such a situation: "I went into a store shopping for a boat, to buy a nice one. I saw one that I liked and then I saw that it had a big engine on it. I asked the dealer how much fuel it used and he said, 'If you're worried about the fuel, you can't afford it.' I just walked out. That's happened before."

Traveling to exotic lands is the dream of many people, but not of many millionaire winners. Twelve reported going on trips after winning. Two families went to the Poconos in Pennsylvania, and four journeyed to Florida. Three winners visited California, and four tried their luck in Las Vegas. Trips to Europe, Hawaii, the Bahamas, Mexico, the Virgin Islands, Jamaica, South America, and an around-the-world cruise were also taken, but only five winners accounted for these more ambitious excursions. Yet even people who traveled relatively short distances enjoyed themselves. For example, a high-school janitor who won $50,000 in the New York State Lottery reminisced: "After I won, we took a vacation. We drove up to Nova Scotia and went to Prince Edward Island. It was the nicest vacation we ever had, and I'm glad the people in the state of New York paid for it."

Only eleven winners had regular vacations before they won, and the most common thing they did was to stay home or travel to the New Jersey shore for a weekend. Eight people never had a formal vacation, and the rest took a couple of days, which they usually spent painting and repairing their houses. Many had not had the opportunity to travel before, and now were unsure where to go. As one fellow put it, "When you're living hand-to-mouth, you never have time to make trips to Florida or California."

But there are other reasons for the dearth of traveling. As the winners learned, it is expensive, especially when families are taken along. One middle-aged widow said longingly, "I'd love to go to Australia, but that's the next million." She had just purchased a $118,000 house. Then, too, traveling with children is often a tedious experience, so many couples opted for nearby places and looked forward to the day when they would be able to travel alone.

Five millionaires wanted to travel more, but were afraid to fly. They hoped to overcome this phobia, but were not actively trying to. One sixty-three-year-old winner figured he would become braver as time went on: "I'm gonna fly after I get a few more checks." Those who refused to fly resorted to cars for trips. Three winners have driven coast to coast twice, and four regularly drive to Florida.

In three families, one spouse wanted to travel but the other did not. Fortunately, the vacation-minded spouse was content to remain home. One nontraveler explained: "My wife wants to travel. She'd like to take a cruise. Her friends want her to go along with them and I told her it's all right, but she won't go without me. So we stay home together."

Travel is also a matter of one's priorities. Most winners placed greater emphasis on obtaining homes. Although they had hoped to visit distant lands, they postponed or abandoned these plans. One winner recalled his fantasy: "I wanted to go to Africa on a picture-taking safari, but I spent the money elsewhere." The remark of a thirty-three-year-c`d millionaire is perhaps more revealing: "I haven't taken any trips and I don't plan to. What makes it any different in Arizona than it is here? It's just warmer. It all depends on your point of view." That is in essence why so many winners have not traveled. Deprived of vacations in the past, they were not prepared socially and psychologically for such experiences.

The prior lives and experiences of winners were also reflected in their leisure and recreational activities. Many millionaires said they had only a few friends, and only thirteen were members of any social, service, or religious organization. Seven engaged in some form of community service work, usually to overcome the boredom of being unemployed. The most common leisure activities were watching television, working around the house, and entertaining at home. Only six people reported going to concerts, two to lectures, four to art galleries or museums, and five to the theater.

Some winners, however, were determined to enrich their lives, and three millionaires enrolled in college. Seventeen-year-old Cheryl Braun was a high-school senior when she won and did not let the notoriety interfere with her career plans. Today she is a college junior majoring in business administration and plans to become a personnel specialist. She is very secretive about winning, and none of her classmates knows.

Penny Ratkowski was just a year older than Cheryl when her parents won $114,000 in the New York State Lottery and gave her and her brother, Robert, each $28,000. She quit her assembly-line job in an electronics factory.

"I was bored so I quit. I took it easy for three months after we won. My mother got mad and threatened to withhold the money. Then I enrolled at a local college. I wanted to major in the performing arts."

Her mother interjected: "She's a talented mezzo. She won

several voice competitions. She was an all-state singer in high school, too. Her voice is so beautiful that people cry when she sings. She had song and dance lessons for eleven years. One of her college teachers was so impressed that she invited her to study in Europe for a year, but with one month to go before the end of her freshman year she quit school."

"Yeah, and it cost me $1,600 of my winnings. I felt it was a waste 'cause what I was studying was the same as high school. Now I'm a sales clerk making $2.10 an hour. I've been working there for three months, but I want to go back to school for nursing to get a future lined up. I want more money—I don't do that much, but I should get more. I'm on my feet all day. I'm still doing the shitty jobs. I wanted to go to college, but we couldn't do it because we didn't have the money. Then when we got it I went and didn't like it anyway. I wanted to go into show business—go to New York and travel, see everything and meet people."

The money is almost gone now, and her mother feels she made a mistake by giving it to the children because her twenty-one-year-old son quit his job, too. He was a salesman and used his share to buy a pickup truck and establish a remodeling company. "He left a good-paying job for that, and now he has no work to do," she said despondently.

Being self-employed is a cornerstone of the American Dream of Success, and three other winners used the money to go into business for themselves. Arthur Andrews was nineteen when his fiancée, Karen, won a million dollars. They were married a few months later, and he left his carpenter's job, invested $3,000 of the winnings in new tools and equipment, and began a mobile-home remodeling company. The hours are long and the work is hard. He averages twelve hours a day, six or seven days a week, and the pay is nothing to brag about (last year he grossed $10,000). But he doesn't mind because he is independent and enjoys it.

Not only millionaires used the money to embark on careers. In New York, Richard Ritter was a sheetmetal worker for eleven years. He is married and the father of four children.

"I mainly installed flashing. I was earning $8.50 an hour at the time I left, but the work was seasonal. I'd work seven months a year, and every winter they laid me off. I average $7,000 to $8,000 a year. I was all the way, all I could do was make the raises."

Then, two years ago, he won $50,000.

"I had a good life before, but it's given us a little more security. I got a break and it gave me a chance to get into something I always wanted a little sooner. I used $32,000 as a down payment on this bar. It's got a restaurant and three bowling alleys, too. My friend owned it. He wanted to give me a chance to get ahead. He knew my resources were limited, so he settled for a minimum down payment."

But now Dick is saddled with huge payments on his $115,000 mortgage, which consume most of his profits. To cut his expenses he moved his family into a small apartment over the bar. He has found, like other self-employed winners, that the responsibilities are many and the work days long.

"I average over a hundred hours a week here, compared with the forty hours I used to work. Before, I could always plan on three to four months off. I have little time for many of the things I used to do since I took this place over, but I like what I'm doing. Now I work from the time I get up till I get a chance to sit down. I get up about ten A.M. and start working in the kitchen. We open at eleven. From six until closing at 3:30 I tend bar. I take care of the alleys, too. On Friday nights we serve over 350 fish dinners, and I've got eleven people to supervise. I'm trying to learn the business, but there's always something popping up. I would say right now it's wearing me down a little bit. I get nervous about things."

One senses that the financial rewards are somewhat less than he expected.

"Everything is put back into it. It's as though I'm not making anything. I don't take any set salary out, but I average about $125 a week. I figure in two years I'll be able to start making something out of it. I expect to make about $20,000 a year in three years. I'm putting more hours in now, but it's for me, not someone else. Ten years from now I'll sell it and invest in something else and take it easier."

Two people, a millionaire and a $200,000 winner (Rita Fortunato, whom we met in Chapter 5), used large amounts to keep their businesses afloat. The former owned a company supplying industrial tool equipment. The recession of the 1970's decreased demand for his services and he laid off his six employees. His wife explained: "The business is going downhill now. If it hadn't been for the money he put into it from the winnings, he probably would have lost it."

Even relatively small amounts of prize money can have a significant impact on people's working lives and standard of living. One of the more interesting illustrations of this occurred in a unique and unexpected place.

Mr. and Mrs. Joseph Price live with their three young children in a trailer which they bought three weeks after winning $50,000 in the New York State Lottery. It is not a lavish residence, hidden in the woods of rural western New York, but to them it is a decided step up. Indeed, they have the distinction of having one of the newest and most modern domiciles where they live—the Tuscarora Indian Reservation.

The reservation stands high on a bluff overlooking the orchards and vineyards of Niagara County. On a clear day you can see the skyscrapers and needle-nose TV tower in Toronto. But the land on the reservation looks barren. Most dwellings are reminiscent of the rural poverty one might find in Appalachia, not adjacent to some of the most lavish homes on the Niagara frontier. On the reservation many homes are unfinished or in a state of disrepair. There are numerous tarpaper shacks and accompanying outhouses, abandoned automobiles, and piles of junk.

Joseph is a full-blooded Seneca Indian, and his wife, Nancy, is half Tuscarora. They have lived all their lives here. Their previous home lacked running water and plumbing, and

Nancy confessed that "things were pretty bad then. I had one child and was pregnant with my second. We were constantly running out of money. It was spent before we even made it."

Even when Joseph, who was then an apprentice roofer, was employed, he earned only $3 an hour. His work was seasonal, and he averaged about $7,000 a year.

Joseph was twenty-five when he won, and he had not thought his life would get much better. Winning came as a complete surprise because the Prices had never bought a lottery ticket. Joseph's mother purchased the ticket in their names, and since then their lives have improved considerably. "I'd say we don't have it as hard as some people do. It pulled us out of debt and helped us to get on our feet," said Nancy.

Before they won, they never had a vacation together, but the summer after winning, they managed to take their children camping for two weeks in the Adirondacks. That was five years ago. Although they would like to do this again, they have not been able to get away since.

"We plan to go to Florida for two weeks, or the Adirondacks again, but our plans will probably fall through as they usually do," complained Nancy. "But, in general, I would say that our lives are much better now than before. We go out more now, usually to a movie. Before, we were very tight. Since then there isn't the strain. The atmosphere has been a lot more relaxed."

With the $29,000 they received after taxes, they paid $1,500 in debts, bought their trailer for $6,000, spent $2,000 for furniture, and bought a new Chevrolet. The car was a necessity since Joseph would sometimes have to travel as much as three hundred miles a day to get to and from a job. They also gave a small amount to Nancy's parents to help them build a house. The remaining $16,000 was given to their eldest son.

Joseph still works as a roofer, but he is now a journeyman earning $8.12 an hour, averaging around $10,000 a year. Despite the addition of Nancy's $6,000 secretarial salary to their family income, they still cannot manage to save, even though they pay only $30 a month for the plot upon which their trailer rests. Although they would like to own land on the reservation, tribal law forbids it. Nancy is not a full-blooded member of the tribe. While they do not plan to live there indefinitely, they feel bound to the tribe and its customs.

"We want our children to have an Indian background," said Nancy, "and living on the reservation is a good way of giving them this. Someday we'll be able to move off the reservation and buy land—not very far from here, though."

Although many winners spoke of buying land, only two invested sizable amounts in real estate other than their homes. As with travel and leisure activities, there have not been many innovative investments. Fifteen millionaires did, however, invest varying amounts. Though stocks are enticing, most winners did not want to press their luck, and only six millionaires bought shares. Two people received professional advice and put considerable sums into the market. A sixty-year-old widow invested $20,000 in a diversified portfolio, and a retired bartender invested $30,000 in a sports complex. Another man invested $20,000 in mutual funds. The other three invested less than $3,000. One lost part of his investment and decided to opt out of the market, while the remaining two are contemplating future investments.

Four millionaires put some winnings in municipal bonds because they considered them a secure, tax-free investment. Two of these people have long-range plans. Bob Whelan's program for investing in bonds spans ten to fifteen years and will be worth upward of $200,000. Salvatore Lenochi is investing $10,000–$15,000 annually in municipal bonds. Both were well informed and received professional advice. However, Walter Johnson was not, and panicked when the bond market received adverse publicity.

"I saw in the papers that if a municipality decided to scrap a project, you'd be stuck with their bonds. You'd have to sell them for whatever you could get. So I cashed them in. I lost

$7,000 on them, but I deducted it from my taxes."

Only nine millionaires had coordinated investment plans. The remainder dabbled in stocks and bonds and spent the bulk of their installments on their huge mortgages and expensive new cars each year. Five millionaires annually banked large sums, and only one put the money in a time savings account, which yields higher interest. For the most part, winners, regardless of the size of their prizes, were reluctant, overly cautious investors.

Aside from purchasing new homes, the largest amount was literally given away. Winners' children were the primary recipients of their largesse. Some people annually subsidized their offspring, while those with younger children set sums aside for their college education. Three winners gave $18,000 to each of their children for down payments on homes. A few people, like Jimmy Siciliano, used the money to lavish gifts on their children.

Other relatives also received money, although their expectations often exceeded the amount they got. Many young winners, such as thirty-three-year-old Ronald Carlson, gave their parents money. "I helped my mother some. My parents were divorced and my mother's remarried. She expects me to give her lots of money. She asked for $8,000. I sent her a couple of hundred and I pay her doctor bills, but her husband is still working. Until he retires and they need it, I'm not going to support them."

Differences between expectations and the actual amounts relatives received sometimes resulted in acrimony. Most winners, however, experienced great satisfaction from giving, especially to their churches. One-time bequests to churches ranged from a few hundred dollars to the $4,000 which Johnnie De Carlo doled out to assorted denominations because he, like many others, believed winning was a gift from God.

Similar sentiments were echoed by Ronald Carlson, who tithes his winnings and annually gives $5,000 to his church. Even winners of small amounts gave between $500 and

$1,500 as gestures of appreciation for what they considered to be divine intervention in their lives.

Perhaps the most vivid illustration of the winners' new financial security was their lack of liabilities. With the exception of mortgages, only one millionaire had an outstanding debt. The others were free of the economic hassles which complicate and frustrate our lives. Paying off debts afforded some previously beleaguered people an opportunity to have some sweet revenge. Wilma Kovaleski recounted the following episode:

"I was a customer for thirty-five years at Bamberger's and I had a charge account there. Things were getting pretty rough, and I couldn't pay the full amount of my bill, so I paid them what I could. I didn't owe that much, anyway. I went there one day to get a pair of shoes, but they wouldn't let me charge them. I was furious. Shortly after this happened, I won and paid them off. Then I sent a letter to the president along with my charge card, which I cut up. I told him what happened and that I just won a million and would never set foot in there again."

Millionaires' assets vary greatly because of differences in spending patterns, investments, employment status, affluence prior to winning, and the number of checks received. Twelve people had received four checks; seven, three; eight, two; and eight, one when they were interviewed. The rough estimates of assets reported by millionaires averaged over $121,000. The largest amount reported was $225,000 by a winner who had received four checks. Contrary to what one might expect, differences in assets between winners who had received several checks and those who had received only one or two were small.

Whether winners' financial holdings will increase depends on the investments they make, their spending patterns, and their ability to seek and learn from competent advice. Most winners were still in a transitional period. Judging from their spending behavior, work experience, and future plans, perhaps twenty of the thirty-five millionaire families will continue to consume the money, relying on it as their primary source of income. Half of them are fifty-five or over and may not live to see the last installment, but what of the rest? Will they begin to react as prisoners on death row, viewing each successive check as one less year to live? Obviously, there will be some adjusting and reassessing, and it is to be hoped that the more liberal spenders will begin to take stock of their situation and invest the money prudently. This is important, because those subsisting exclusively on their installments no longer work, and only three will have pensions.

Despite their trepidation, the harassment, tax problems, and conflicts with friends and relatives, no one regretted having won or wanted to give the money back. Indeed, nearly all the winners still buy tickets and hope to win again. Even those who had negative experiences felt the money had given them security, relieved the financial burdens of life, and provided an opportunity to start anew. Only time will tell whether they will take advantage of the opportunities afforded by their gifts.

About the Author

H. ROY KAPLAN was born in Newark, New Jersey. He received his Ph.D. from the University of Massachusetts in 1971 and is currently Associate Professor of Sociology at the State University of New York at Buffalo. Dr. Kaplan is a specialist in the sociology of work, a topic on which he has written numerous articles and edited a book, *American Minorities and Economic Opportunity*. He has recently completed a study of million-dollar lottery winners in Canada.

Dr. Kaplan lives with his wife and their two sons in Snyder, New York. He is a vegetarian, jogs six to seven miles a day, and is a habitual lottery-ticket loser.